Tender Violence in US Schools is a provocative book that provides a critical genealogy of the white woman teacher imagined as the heroic savior of children of color. Rooted in nineteenth-century settler colonial missionizing, Bauer persuasively argues that a gendered discourse of "benevolent whiteness" continues to unjustly shape education today. Such teacher-savior narratives erase the love and learning Black and Native children receive from their own communities. With historic examples from Hawai'i, South Carolina, and Dakota-Sioux Territory, alongside the contemporary Teach for America program, Bauer calls for a deep reckoning with the structural violence of education. A must-read for scholars in Education, Ethnic, Indigenous and Gender Studies.

Maile Arvin, Assistant Professor of Gender Studies and History, University of Utah, and author of *Possessing Polynesians: The Science of Settler Colonial Whiteness in Hawai'i and Oceania*

Tender Violence in US Schools offers a vivid critical genealogy of white women teachers grounded in a social history of missionization through three nineteenth-century case studies across diverse geographies – Hawai'i, the Sea Islands off the coast of Georgia and South Carolina, and Dakota Sioux Territory. Interrogating the self-constructed discourse of white women's selflessness and self-proclaimed heroism, this compelling study offers a robust theory of "benevolent whiteness" to understand education as a tool for settler colonial and white supremacist control vis-à-vis Indigenous and Black students in order to challenge this formation as it is still endemic to US schooling into the present.

J. Kēhaulani Kauanui, Professor of American Studies, Wesleyan University, and author of *Paradoxes of Hawaiian Sovereignty*

If we really want to address racial and gender inequality in education, we need to dig deep into the history of the teaching profession. *Tender Violence* does just that, interrogating the cherished trope of the teacher-as-savior. A provocation, this book offers a genealogy of benevolent whiteness in US schooling and shows us how feminized white supremacy gets replicated in the present. Bauer calls all who care about education to confront these histories and to open space for Black and Indigenous community visions. Essential reading for current and future teachers and school leaders!

Noelani Goodyear-Ka'ōpua, Professor of Political Science, University of Hawai'i at Mānoa, and author of *The Seeds We Planted: Portraits of a Native Hawaiian Charter School*

TENDER VIOLENCE IN US SCHOOLS

Within educational research, the over-disciplining of Black and Indigenous students is most often presented as a problem located within pathologized or misunderstood communities. That is, theories and proposed solutions tend toward those that ask how we can make students of color from particular backgrounds more suited to US educational standards rather than questioning the racist roots of those standards. *Tender Violence in US Schools* takes as a provocation this "discipline gap," in exploring a thus far unconsidered stance and asking how white women (the majority of US teachers) have historically understood their roles in the disciplining of Black and Indigenous students, and how and why their role has been constructed over time and space in service to institutions of the white settler colonial state.

Natalee Kēhaulani Bauer (Kanaka ʻŌiwi) is Department Chair of Race, Gender, & Sexuality Studies at Mills College in Oakland, CA.

Indigenous and Decolonizing Studies in Education
Series Editors: Eve Tuck and K. Wayne Yang

Indigenous and Decolonizing Studies in Education
Mapping the Long View
edited by Linda Tuhiwai-Smith, Eve Tuck, and K. Wayne Yang

Applying Indigenous Research Methods
Storying with Peoples and Communities
edited by Sweeney Windchief and Timothy San Pedro

Indigenous Children's Survivance in Public Schools
Leilani Sabzalian

Decolonizing Place in Early Childhood Education
Fikile Nxumalo

Education in Movement Spaces
Standing Rock to Chicago Freedom Square
edited by Alayna Eagle Shield, Django Paris, Rae Paris, and Timothy San Pedro

Urban Indigenous Youth Reframing Two-Spirit
Marie Laing

Tender Violence in US Schools
Benevolent Whiteness and the Dangers of Heroic White Womanhood
Natalee Kēhaulani Bauer

For more information about this series, please visit: https://www.routledge.com/ Indigenous-and-Decolonizing-Studies-in-Education/book-series/IDSE

TENDER VIOLENCE IN US SCHOOLS

Benevolent Whiteness and
the Dangers of Heroic White
Womanhood

Natalee Kēhaulani Bauer

Routledge
Taylor & Francis Group

NEW YORK AND LONDON

Cover artwork by Malia Hulleman

First published 2023
by Routledge
605 Third Avenue, New York, NY 10158

and by Routledge
4 Park Square, Milton Park, Abingdon, Oxon, OX14 4RN

Routledge is an imprint of the Taylor & Francis Group, an informa business

© 2023 Natalee Kēhaulani Bauer

ISBN: 978-1-032-06337-9 (hbk)
ISBN: 978-1-032-06336-2 (pbk)
ISBN: 978-1-003-20180-9 (ebk)

DOI: 10.4324/9781003201809

Typeset in Bembo
by SPi Technologies India Pvt Ltd (Straive)

CONTENTS

EDITORS' FOREWORD

Here is our humble prediction. You are going to want to gift this book to a lot of people. You will read it, and it will remind you of someone, and you will want to share it with them. It might be a fond remembrance, a remembrance of solidarity as classmates in someone's classroom, a classroom tinged with the "loving" violence of benevolent whiteness. It might be a scornful remembrance, a remembrance of having just barely survived. You will read this book and want to send this to the teachers who might understand their role, their labor, their presence, the profession that they have inherited, as otherwise. You will read this book, and want to send it out to the world.

Natalee Kēhaulani Bauer, in writing *Tender Violence in US Schools: Benevolent Whiteness and the Dangers of Heroic White Womanhood*, joins a community of scholars who have long been interrogating the roles of whiteness and white womanhood in what we have come to understand as the profession of teaching. Other scholars in this community, including Bree Picower (2009) and Madeline Grumet (1988), have attended to ways that the profession of teaching has emerged from a particular history of entrenched whiteness (Picower) and the dialectic of public-private of reproductive work (Grumet). Bauer's book joins this conversation in an expansive way, bringing to the table a comprehensive analysis of the roles of white women teachers in settler colonialism, and the specificities of loving violence that have shaped the profession of teaching. It makes us think of Stephanie Jones-Rogers (2019) and research in Black studies about the menacing presence of white women enslavers. It makes us think of Aileen Moreton-Robinson (2021) and other Indigenous scholars who wrestle with white feminisms.

Bauer analyzes confessional writings by white women teachers. These sometimes I-narratives that Bauer engages are not minor accounts, but national best sellers in their times. They are missionary accounts that influenced the discourses of the goals, disposition, and comportment of teachers; importantly, these confessional writings also influenced the discourses about their students, contributing to the perpetual trope of the student from whom white women need protection. These accounts promote the image of the exceptional white heroine saving multitudes of dark faces with the grace of the schoolhouse, often against her own subordination in American patriarchy. The desires expressed in writings by pioneering white women teachers often include a thirst for heroic recognition as well as for equality in power to white men. Bauer shows how women missionary educators contributed to anti-Indigenous and anti-Black US empire through a feminized register of white supremacy – one that drew on domestic discourses of the private sphere such as mothering and nurturing. She does so through an analysis of their texts, memoirs, and biographies, the continued circulation of which has generated a public discourse about schooling that is feminized maternal even while it is paternalistic. In this way, Bauer makes legible the ways that missionary attitudes toward teaching have given way to schooling structures that pathologize and control poor students, and students of color and their families, while preserving the bodily and emotional safety of white women.

Nonetheless, this is not a book about white women, nor is Bauer's analysis exclusive of nonwhite teachers. Rather, in theorizing benevolent whiteness, she draws our attention to the gendered-and-raced mutability of white supremacy. People invested in the schooling mission can reproduce the power dynamics of benevolent whiteness whether they identify as white or not. Teacher education is susceptible to this particular hidden curriculum. Thus, one aspect of this book that reverberates with us is the interiority of the feminized heroine in the context of a patriarchal nation. The private-public nature of the schoolteacher means that her role is to move in this or that way, to adjust to a patriarchal structure, then to teach (our) children to do it too.

The book's cover art is gorgeous. To us, it invokes this intimacy of education – as intimate as the laps of adult family members reading to their children. Yet, it also reclaims this relationship back from the loving violence of colonial schooling. The images of Indigenous adults and children reading together resist the dominant portrait of the white woman teaching literacy. Perhaps they are unlearning together the myths of benevolent whiteness, in order to protect future Indigenous schoolchildren from its harms. Perhaps they are reading ancestor stories about an Indigenous future. As Bauer reminds us, Indigenous education existed before and beyond the heroic arrival of missionary schoolteachers, and "Black schooling was everywhere, and it was valued beyond measure as the key to an entire people's emancipation."

We also see the immense potential for the interventions made in this book for how we understand the future of the profession of teaching. In arguing that teaching in the United States can be transformed by moving out of the continuous loop of individual heroism, Bauer points to a profession that does more than uphold settler colonialism. In unsettling the conflation of teaching and exceptional heroism, more theories of change for the practice of teaching can proliferate.

This is a book that will feel familiar to many readers, even though it is a unique contribution. She does the heavy lifting work to provide evidence for that which many schooled communities know all too deeply. Bauer conducts a careful audit of the narratives that are foundational to the expansion of missionary schools into Indigenous nations and Black communities, and almost like a geometric proof, lays bare the invisibilized power cords that we know are there, but to which we cannot point. Perhaps Bauer wrote this book so you would not have to do this same heavy lifting. Often, this well-worn narrative overwhelms the space for the conversations that we want to have about schooling, namely, conversations rooted in Indigenous epistemologies, Black education for liberation, a path forward from the pathways that have always been. This book makes space for other purposes of teaching and schooling to get some air and sunshine.

Perhaps you are the one who has been gifted this book. If so, we hope that you can regard it for the gift it is: a corrective on the practices of teaching that are undergirded by white supremacy and settler colonialism; a healing balm to the gaslighting that can punctuate the experiences of children and youth in classrooms defined by benevolent whiteness.

Eve Tuck & K. Wayne Yang

References

Grumet, M. R. (1988). *Bitter milk: Women and teaching*. Amherst: University of Massachusetts.

Jones-Rogers, S. E. (2019). *They were her property*. London: Yale University Press.

Moreton-Robinson, A. (2021). *Talkin'up to the white woman: Indigenous women and feminism*. Minneapolis, MN: University of Minnesota Press.

Picower, B. (2009). The unexamined whiteness of teaching: How white teachers maintain and enact dominant racial ideologies. *Race Ethnicity and Education*, 12(2), 197–215.

NĀ MAHALO/ACKNOWLEDGMENTS

My gratitude at this moment is overwhelming. I have been fortunate beyond measure during the decade-plus it has taken to write this book. I have had incredible peers, advisors, informal mentors, friends, family, students, professors, former teachers, colleagues, and Academic-Twitter-strangers-turned-interlocutors who have made this project possible and who consistently reminded me of its value and necessity. We should all be so lucky to have such a community.

To begin, I want to recognize that the writing of this book in its current and earlier form as my doctoral dissertation, as well as the coursework and research leading up to it, took place on stolen lands still inhabited by and rightfully belonging to Indigenous peoples. On the continent this work took place in Huchiun, in unceded Lisjan territory currently known as Oakland and Berkeley, California. Additionally, archival research and early drafting of the dissertation took place in my homeland, on the island of Oʻahu. There is a strange and incommensurable feeling of both gratitude and trauma to have done this particular work on these lands, as both settler and dispossessed. I am grateful to the community I've found in both places, particularly for the ongoing encouragement that this book needed to be written for all of us. I am also deeply grateful that these Indigenous peoples, these mana wāhine, and multiple generations of radical Black women in the Bay have become part of the larger village/lāhui that surrounds my children and models for them our interdependence, our shared struggles, and, most importantly, our uninterrupted and beautiful resistance and resilience through centuries of US violence that would rather (but could never) erase us.

I have had substantial support and encouragement, from graduate school to my current career, and I am painfully aware of how rare this is for queer and Indigenous women in academia. As a doctoral student, I was taught and mentored exclusively by professors of color, predominantly women, in the Social and Cultural Studies program in the Graduate School of Education (GSE) at the University of California at Berkeley. Na'ilah Suad Nasir, Janelle Scott, and Michael Dumas were always willing to stop and chat in passing, answer emails, or invite me into their offices for conversation; there was always time for me and my ideas, in varying states of clarity – someone who was not even their student – and for that I am grateful. Zeus Leonardo led our cohort in its first yearlong seminar, which we left each week feeling as intellectually exhausted as we were inspired. As a fellow lover of language and literary allusions, he taught me that even the most complex theoretical writing can be as poetic as it is incisive. Finally, my doctoral adviser, Lisa García Bedolla, continues to be a consistent source of knowledge, support, humor, and unwavering faith in me. Thank you for trusting me to take big leaps and to work things out on my own, but always knowing when and how to rein me in when the nets I cast were far too large to catch anything of value. Thank you for reminding me that family is the most important thing, and for holding me accountable academically, while also holding space (often literally) for me to continue on this path with my babies in tow. More than anything, thank you for "gently nudging me" to return to *this* work, to what I love and what sustains me, when I felt like I had to change to be the same kind of researcher and scholar as everyone else around me. I am deeply grateful to you for all of this, and for so much more.

Also at Berkeley, professors and colleagues in the Designated Emphasis in Gender, Women, and Sexuality (DEWGS) provided a home outside of my GSE home and an important connection to brilliant colleagues in disciplines across the campus. It was through this program that I discovered the concept of interdisciplinary research, allowing my own work to find its place and become legible in a way that did not require losing parts of itself/myself. The 2014 DEWGS Dissertation Research Seminar with Mel Chen was a much-needed space for peer review, conversation, critique, and acknowledging our limitations, fears, frustrations – our humanity. Within the DEWGS, I am indebted to Paola Bacchetta and Juana María Rodriguez for their kindhearted support, advice, and profound knowledge, which have steadily continued now years past my time as a graduate student. In Ethnic Studies, Michael Omi kindly answered an email from an unknown and anxious student asking to discuss my then very amorphous dissertation proposal. Michael generously agreed to supervise my dissertation, offering to be "whatever I need him to be" on this journey. Michael, your profound wisdom is only matched by your immeasurable kindness and generosity. I am so deeply grateful for the gift of your time, your insight, and your presence.

My cohort in Social and Cultural Studies, Mara Chavez-Diaz, Jocyl Sacramento, Arianna Morales, Tadashi Dozono, and unofficial cohort-mate Ziza Delgado, brought camaraderie and joy to a place that is otherwise known to be highly competitive and individualistic. Outside of my own cohort, there was not a student in the GSE who showed anything less than generosity and love for the work we all do, in our own divergent ways. Of particular note, Connie Wun, Aaminah Norris, Tia Madkins, Funie Hsu, Nirali Jani, Genevieve Negron-Gonzalez, Dinorah Sanchez, Derrika Hunt, David C. Turner, III, Theresa Stone, Christyna Serrano-Crenshaw, José Ramón Lizárraga, and Arturo Cortez are just a few radical scholars of color who were (and often still are) always a text away for advice, critique, commiserating, and conspiring about everything from parenting to publication.

Mahalo nui e Hinemoana of Turtle Island, nā mana wāhine, Liza Keanuenueokalani Williams, Lani Teves, Fuifuilupe Niumetolu, Kēhaulani Vaughn, and Maile Arvin; mahalo piha for consistently reassuring me that my work was both interesting and important, and for generously reading any draft or idea I sent your way. To the Kanaka wāhine senior scholars who answered cold email requests, and whose work opened eyes and doors – Noenoe Silva, Noe Goodyear-Kaʻōpua, Lisa Kahaleole Hall, and especially J. Kēhaulani Kauanui, who generously took me on as a cross-country mentee, lighting a much needed fire under me in my last year of writing the dissertation and who has been a consistent mentor as I navigate early career academia. The initial proposal for this book was the result of her willingness to guide me step-by-step through the process of proposing my first manuscript when that process seemed indecipherable. The more I speak to other Kanaka scholars, the more I realize Kēhaulani has been this person for so many of us. Mahalo palena ʻole iā ʻoe e Kēhaulani – your generosity is without limits, and is the model for the type of scholar, mentor, and human I aspire to be.

I would not be the scholar I am today if it weren't for the students, staff, and faculty at Mills College in Oakland, California, where I completed my undergraduate and master's degrees in English and where I am now faculty and Chair of the Race, Gender, and Sexuality Studies (RGSS) Department. As a graduate student in English Literature, I drank in the brilliance of Cynthia Scheinberg, Diane Cady, Elmaz Abinader, Ajuan Mance, Kim Magowan, Vivian Chin, Tom Strychacz, and Rebekah Edwards, whose intellectual rigor, generosity, and encouragement first made me see myself as a potential scholar and peer. They have been lifelong mentors, and now many of them are colleagues down the hall. Kirsten Saxton is also included in this group of phenomenal mentor-colleagues, though she deserves special acknowledgment and appreciation. My graduate advisor, professor, thesis supervisor, lifelong application reviewer, writer of countless letters of recommendation, always-available editor, advisor, interlocutor, cheerleader, and most importantly my friend: I am so indebted to you, all the pages in this book could not begin to contain an appropriate measure of gratitude. At your request, I daily demonstrate my gratitude for you by emulating your inexhaustible generosity and profound love for students and teaching.

In the Women, Gender, & Sexuality Studies (WGSS) program at Mills, Priya Kandaswamy, Brinda Mehta, Judith Bishop, and Margo Okazawa-Rey have been exceptional mentors and colleagues, always reminding me to prioritize my own work, family, and sanity. Their gentle nudges of "how's that book coming?" kept me accountable when the problem solver in me wanted to focus solely on students and the chaos we've been living through. Priya, not a day goes by that I don't miss you and try to imagine what you'd do if you were in my shoes (now that I am left filling yours). I'm so grateful for the kindness and humanity you modeled as department chair and as a friend. Mills was a better place with you a part of it. In both WGSS and Ethnic Studies, I have been given the freedom and trust to grow as a scholar and leader, thanks to the opportunity provided by Chinyere Oparah and the faith and camaraderie of my colleagues mentioned above as well as Lorena Muñoz, Patricia St. Onge, Amy Argenal, Susan Stryker, Lisa Arellano, Rebekah Edwards, and department administrator extraordinaire, Zamora. I am also particularly grateful to my Ethnic Studies colleague Susan Ito for her immeasurable kindness and support, whether through reading drafts, delivering home baked treats, leaving notes of encouragement on my office door, or sending flowers to celebrate the mini victories along the road to completing this manuscript. It is a rare and humbling experience to be surrounded by humans who graciously hold such balanced brilliance and generosity.

I am especially lucky to be affiliated with the Mills College School of Education (SOE), whose commitment to antiracism, liberation, justice, and joy is an exemplar for the rest of the College and the larger academic and educational world. Dean of the SOE, Wendi Williams, has been my go-to person for thinking through hard situations with students or as a faculty leader. Along with Dean Williams, my SOE Faculty Village neighbors and colleagues, Wanda Watson, Dana Wright, Jonathan Iris-Wilbanks, Pedro Nava, Argelia Lara, and their families provided community, joy, and laughter during the most uncertain of pandemic times. They've also remained generous collaborators, readers of drafts, sounding boards, and trusted friends. I am particularly indebted to Wanda Watson and Pedro Nava, early colleague-friends and supporters from my pre-faculty days, for allowing me to sneak my first foot into the door of this exceptional SOE community.

My colleagues across the Mills campus make coming to work a gift, even as we enter year three of a global pandemic, and as we navigate the unknown future of a potential merger with a much larger research university. The uncertainty of our current situation has brought out the best in my colleagues and gives me renewed faith in what can be achieved even within historically white institutions of higher education. There are far too many to name, but please trust that I consider it a unique gift and a privilege to work alongside all of you.

At Mills I have been lucky to mentor brilliant undergraduate student researchers Mariana Sauceda, Katherine Funes, Chiany Dri, and Sage Madans, all of whom furthered this project through thoughtful conversation and analysis, and more practically speaking through transcription of often-translucent old texts written in 19th-century cursive and the more tedious tasks of searching through the text for missing or extraneous citations. In its earliest incarnation, this project was also supported by student research assistants Pūlama Long in Hawaiʻi, Cheyenne Linet Palaico-McCarthy in Massachusetts, and Ifechukwu Okeke in Berkeley, whose work made this multi-archival project possible.

Much appreciation is owed to the archivists who contributed to this project's success. Dore Minatodani, Senior Librarian in the Hawaiian Collection at the University of Hawaiʻi at Mānoa, offered me my first introduction into, and guidance around, conducting archival research. Archivists at the Hawaiian Mission Childrens' Society library (HMCS), Amistad Research Center at Tulane University, and the Eastman-Goodale-Dayton Family Papers in Sophia Smith Collection at Smith College are owed much gratitude for their aid in my navigation of the archives as a scholar new to this type of research.

As a doctoral student at UC Berkeley where this book was born, I received generous financial support, including the Chancellor's Fellowship that allowed me four years of focused academic work time, and the Dissertation Completion Fellowship, which provided an additional year of funding while writing the dissertation. In my final three years at Berkeley, the Graduate Division Student Parent Grant helped subsidize childcare expenses, allowing me to maintain a productive daily writing schedule while my children were well taken care of. Finally, the UC Berkeley Center for Race and Gender awarded me two Graduate Student Research Grants that helped to pay stipends to student research assistants across the country making this multi-archival project possible. In the final years of drafting the manuscript, the Meg Quigley Faculty Research Fellowship and Summer Research Grant at Mills College provided me course releases and small stipends to pay for summer childcare, additional student research assistants, and editors, among other expenses. Also at Mills, the Research Justice at the Intersections fellowship (2019–2020) provided the time and intellectual conversation needed to focus on this work while also balancing teaching full time and life in general.

Many thanks to my editor, Leslie Castro Woodhouse at Origami Editorial, and my editor at Routledge, Jessica Cooke, for their support in making this book possible. Additionally, I am profoundly grateful to this series' editors Eve Tuck and K. Wayne Yang for their generous and generative feedback throughout the many revisions of this manuscript as we all simultaneously navigate parenthood, academia, kuleana, and life in general during a years-long global pandemic.

Mahalo piha to aloha ʻāina Malia Hulleman for the beautiful cover art created especially for this book, and for her persistent reminders that this is for the lāhui.

Finally, to my family both by birth and by choice, especially my children Kainoa Joseph and Keala Nākoa: everything is for you, and none of this would have been possible without you.

INTRODUCTION

One of the most persistent and dangerous tropes about teaching in the United States is that it is an act of individual heroism. In US popular culture we are inundated with memoirs, movies, and viral videos celebrating the individual teacher and their capacity to save individual "problem" students, and therefore by extension to "solve" the problems of educational and social systems. An individualized teacher/savior narrative ignores the systemic and structural foundation of schooling, instead centering the exceptional individual teacher as the solution to systemic problems. This narrative lacks an analysis of the racialized political, social, and economic contexts within which schools are located. This overarchingly problematic narrative is particularly dangerous because of the virtually unexamined history of gendered white supremacy that shaped and continues to inform it. The trope of teachers as heroes is entangled in settler colonial histories of white women teachers, resulting in the data that show that, despite a steady increase in students of color in the United States, our teachers remain predominantly white and female, a statistic that has been true since the formalization of schooling in the mid-19th century.

Relatedly important, in educational research, the over-disciplining of Black[1] and Indigenous students is most often presented as a problem located within pathologized or misunderstood communities. That is, theories and proposed solutions tend toward those that ask how we can make students of color more suited to US educational standards rather than questioning the racist roots of those standards. This book, thus, takes as a provocation this "discipline gap,"[2] and asks how white women (who compose the majority of US teachers) have historically understood and amplified their roles in the disciplining (in both the literal and Foucauldian sense) of Black and Indigenous students, and how and

DOI: 10.4324/9781003201809-1

why their role has been constructed over time and space in service to institutions of the white settler colonial state.

In this book, I explore the culturally violent roots of the popular trope of the exceptional heroic white woman teacher. The following three chapters provide the histories behind these contemporary narratives to demonstrate how they reduce complex educational contexts to ahistorical personal salvation stories of women who magically reach/teach children of color in a way that, presumably, no other teacher (implicitly no teacher of color) could have. These contemporary narratives are national best sellers devoured by early career teachers as a kind of instructional manual, and often chosen as required reading in the very preparation programs that should be working to actively dispel the reductive fairy tale of their simplistically heroic futures that lie ahead. These narratives justify a belief in the inherent pathology of poor Black and Indigenous communities and reinforce our imagining of the heavy but necessary "white [wo]man's burden" to save these communities.

In truth, schools and communities are not waiting for Superman, Michelle Pfeiffer, or Hillary Swank[3] to magically show up one day and begin the process of our salvation. Despite the prevailing narrative, teaching, and particularly teaching poor children of color, is not in itself a heroic act. This is not to say that teaching is easy, nor is it meant to dispute the belief that most teachers arrive at their careers with benevolent intentions. One could argue that in fact most present-day teachers have entered the profession out of a genuine desire to "do good"; yet many teacher education students arrive at our training programs with a well-defined, predetermined understanding of what "good" education looks like, regardless of where and to whom the good is being done. However, to view the teaching of students of color as an act of heroism is not only categorically false, it also does irreparable damage to students, their families, and their communities. The goal of this book then is to add nuance to our understanding of teaching as inherently and always only benevolent, innocent, and heroic.

Reimagining a Layered Methodology

This book is a bit of a paradox, perhaps, in the western imagining of academic texts and historical analysis. While I rely on tools from traditional historical methods, such as literary and discourse analysis, and traditional archival research, my epistemic framework is grounded in Indigenous methodology and an understanding of the power of discourse and storytelling. It is not, however, the type of counternarrative storytelling that is understood as a decolonizing methodology or a recentering of voices of the oppressed or silenced – that work will more easily come after this necessary theorization of benevolent whiteness. Instead, to destabilize what we have collectively come to understand as the truth, I build upon Indigenous understandings of the power of words and stories and the related knowledge that those who control narratives create "truth." Ultimately, I

make this choice with the explicit goal of making visible that which has historically been hidden or normalized, coded as loving intentions, and excused from
answerability. While this book centers the stories of white womanhood, it does
so only to highlight whiteness as not something normative or heroic, but as persistently violent and influential in the formation and ongoing legacy of schooling
in the United States.

Rather than telling the history of 19th-century Black and Indigenous education from the perspective of Black and Indigenous students and teachers, the
focus of this book is to use white women's own words to interrogate and refuse
the narrative that missionary teachers in the 19th century were inherently heroic
or that schools and schooling needed to be brought to places and communities
where in fact those things had a rich history. It seeks to make visible the benevolently violent inspirations behind the massive missionary influx to the places
where Blackness and Indigeneity needed to be controlled, and delineates the
ways in which benevolent whiteness reinforces white supremacy, ideologically
and subtly, through the feminized and loving role of missionary women teachers.
Thus, this book argues for making clear the difference between authentic loving
desires behind education for emancipation versus the false "loving desires" of
benevolent whiteness at play in education for Americanization, indoctrination,
capitalism, and white supremacy. In other words, to make visible the difference
between education as a tool for a people to gain control over their own futures
versus as a tool for controlling a people in perpetuity.

In this book, I offer a genealogical analysis of what I have named "benevolent whiteness": the self-imposed selfless service and heroic identity of white
womanhood in relation to people of color through systematic schooling as the
feminized arm of white supremacy. To do this, I build upon the methodological approaches of Kanaka scholars J. Kēhaulani Kauanui (2018, pp. 30–31) and
'Umi Perkins (2019, p. 69) using a comparative genealogical approach by putting
Foucauldian genealogy and the Kanaka 'Ōiwi methodology of mo'okū'auhau
(loosely translated to English as "genealogy") in conversation with each other to
bridge ideas, understand subjectivity through power/mana, and trace the discursive conditions of the emergence of white womanhood as an inherently benevolent subject, specifically in schooling. Both Foucauldian and Kanaka genealogical
methods focus on power (mana) in unique but complementary ways, Perkins
explains, and thus "It is with this acknowledgment of the role of power that
mo'okū'auhau and Nietzchean and Foucauldian genealogies come into reso-
nance ... they are assertion of the same types of power that are concerned with
the right to rule" (Perkins, 2019, p. 73). Perkins further expounds on the complexity and importance of mo'okū'auhau citing *Native Lands and Foreign Desires:
Pehea lā e pono ai?* (Kame'eleihiwa 1992), "genealogies also brought Hawaiians
comfort in times of acute distress (1992, p. 20).

Building on these understandings of mo'okū'auhau, I attempt to expand
its methodological power to propose that genealogies can also be used to

discomfort – in this case to discomfort whiteness and to unsettle heroic white womanhood. In this manner, I propose, they can be used to rewrite cultural memory, and the false nostalgia of a romanticized heyday of fair and equitable public schooling. In this way, we might argue that Indigenous methodologies such as moʻokūʻauhau, and what Perkins refers to as comparative genealogies, are one way in which we can take down the masters' houses with their own tools after all. In other words, if women's confessional literature was an intentional and powerful tool in reinforcing settler genealogies and futurities, using those texts/ tools to instead deconstruct discourses and power is a way in which Indigenous methodologies destabilize and reject settler colonial narratives of our past and interrupts settler futurity.

In conversation with moʻokūʻauhau as methodology, a Foucauldian-inspired genealogical[4] method is useful in that it asks not what a thing-in-itself was like in history, but how we came to thinking of certain behaviors and actions as *constituting the thing* – in other words, analyzing how the thing (madness, sexuality, benevolent whiteness) was formed discursively by starting with the present understanding of "the thing." Further, Foucault's rejections of traditional linear historical methods teach us that the goal of the genealogical method is not to find fact, nor a "timeless and essential secret, but that [things] have no essence or that their essence was fabricated in a piecemeal fashion from alien forms" (1977, p. 142). This chapter introduces such a genealogical analysis used throughout the book to uncover how we came to define and understand white women teachers as heroes and how such an understanding works both to mask the emotional and ideological violence of schooling and normalize it in such a way that no one is to blame. From that understanding we can ask, what are the contemporary implications of benevolent whiteness, particularly given that the majority of public-school teachers are white women? And further, how does the hero discourse interfere with teacher accountability and their ability to see and locate structural racism as it presents itself in teachers' behaviors and school rules, policies, and so on? How has the disciplining (in both the literal and Foucauldian senses) of kids of color become heroic, and for whom? What purpose does this heroism serve on a larger scale?

To construct this genealogy, in the three main chapters of the book (2–4) I situate historical patterns of benevolent whiteness to then theorize contemporary schooling as an uninterrupted project of gendered white supremacy. To make sense of these historical patterns and draw lines of continuity from the missionary era to the present, I expand on the idea of the "Great White Mother" (Jacobs, 2005, 2009) to introduce my theory of "benevolent whiteness" as a gendered historical and cultural production via the relationship between "middle classness," anti-Blackness, and settler colonialism. I also explore the chronology of and impetus for the "white woman's burden": the feminized counterpart to Kipling's (1899) colonial white man obligated to save an always un-savable people, and the deeper implications of this trope and its role in serving whiteness. It is my hope that, once we examine the genealogy of benevolent whiteness, we are finally able to see the structural and ideological realities that ensure the racialized discipline gap in contemporary US schools as a necessary function of upholding and reproducing white supremacy.

In theorizing benevolent whiteness, I rely on Foucault's concept of disciplinary power (Foucault, 1977) – specifically his theorization of a "gentler" way of controlling society via normalizing judgment of internal monitoring in place of public and physical punishment. In other words, I apply this conceptual framework of "gentler" internal monitoring to the affective control so associated with the "maternal white savior" model of educator I outline above. I also rely on the ways in which Brodhead (1988) uses Foucault's work to theorize "disciplinary intimacy" within the creation of the first public (common) school movement, and I connect this notion of disciplinary intimacy with the feminization of teaching and disciplining. I understand all of this through a genealogical understanding of the dialectical relationship between innocent and at-risk white womanhood and dangerous Black masculinity to lay the foundation for an understanding of benevolent whiteness as a tool of settler colonialism and white supremacy.

Throughout this book, I use analytical tools from settler colonial theory and feminist of color theory to inform my epistemological framing of power as a site of multidimensionality existing across space and depth (Sandoval, 2000) and comprising mutually constructed systems of oppression (Collins, 2002). I apply these lenses to my analysis of women's confessional literature of the 19th century, along with a thorough historical, social, and political understanding of the workings of the State at the time these women were writing and teaching. Although this book aims to uncover the heretofore unacknowledged power and agency of white women within educational reform movements of the 19th century, Black Feminist Thought offers a framework of intersectionality (Crenshaw, 1991) with which to understand middle-class white women's positioning as both oppressed (by patriarchy) and oppressor (within white supremacy). In other words, it is imperative to acknowledge that the 19th-century women's "power and agency" to which I refer throughout this project is limited by its situation within the much larger structure of patriarchal power. Thus, a nuanced analysis of white women's power in the 19th century necessitates an understanding of their complicity in white supremacy as a requirement of escaping some (yet not all) of the limitations of New England Protestant patriarchy. Elaine Moreton-Robinson's newly revised revolutionary book *Talkin' Up to the White Woman: Aboriginal Women and Feminism* (2021) is particularly instructive in this regard, offering a lens through which we can understand the subjective experience of, and power held by white middle-class women in settler colonial states. Moreton-Robinson's critique demonstrates how, through their discursive insistence on identifying themselves as universal unraced-but-gendered humans, white feminists participate in reinscribing racial dominance, all the while concerning themselves intellectually and politically with theorizing oppression and power relations. Through such discourse white women position themselves as wholly disempowered under patriarchy, unwilling participants in racialized power relations, despite their being inextricably connected to and benefitting from whiteness. Whereas Moreton-Robinson uses Indigenous women's voices to "unmask power relations" and "reveal white women's involvement in gendered and racial oppression" (p. 180), I aim to make visible the ways in which white women's voices cover up their participation in racialized and gendered power relations, and yet can be used to unmask and reveal their complicity as well.

In *Tender Violence*, I aspire to build on and be in conversation with Indigenous women scholars like Moreton-Robinson, particularly in the understanding of our intellectual contributions as extensions of "communal responsibility" – our kuleana, to use the most analogous term in 'Ōlelo Hawai'i – that drives this work. This reframing of audience and intergenerational Indigenous knowledge and responsibility reminds me, as it should remind the reader, that although white women are the subject under analysis in this book, they are not meant to be its primary beneficiaries. That is simply not where my kuleana resides.

To construct a genealogy of benevolent whiteness, this book relies on two main methodologies: (1) literary methods, including close textual analysis, and (2) discourse analysis (informed by both Foucault and the field of historical anthropology) which I use in tracing the discursive construction of heroic white womanhood. Following Foucault, I ask how and why a specifically gendered benevolent whiteness has been "put into discourse," and what effects that has had over time in constructing normative ideas and beliefs about the relationship between white female teachers and students of color. I do this by analyzing three main historical archives that span the globe and several decades within the 19th century with a precise focus on the missionary roots of what would become our contemporary US educational system. I analyzed several hundred digitally archived documents including newspapers, letters, diaries, pamphlets, and public records located in the Hawaiian Mission Houses Historic Site and Archives under the auspices of the Hawaiian Mission Children's Society (HMCS) in Honolulu, Hawai'i, and in the Eastman-Goodale-Dayton Family Papers, located in the Sophia Smith Collection at Smith College in Northampton, Massachusetts, and archives of the American Missionary Association and the Amistad Research Center at Tulane University in New Orleans. In addition to analysis of archival documents for a wholistic understanding of white missionary women in the 19th century, in this book I focus each chapter on one of three specific women who each represent different decades and geographies of missionary teaching: Lucy Goodale Thurston in the Kingdom of Hawai'i, Laura Matilda Towne in the Sea Islands off the coast of Georgia and South Carolina, and Elaine Goodale Eastman in Dakota Sioux Territory. I focus on these women specifically because of the volume of writings they left behind and more importantly because their letters and diaries were published as full-length books, two of which (Thurston's and Eastman's) were published by the women themselves.

Rather than using these women's writings to give voice yet again to whiteness, I conduct close readings of their journals and letters and use their own words to tell the story of the discursive construction of benevolent white womanhood with a re-centered focus on whiteness following Leonardo (2009) re-centering whiteness as a means of shining light on its normative nature. Focusing on women's confessional literature (diaries, memoirs, letters) as an archive sheds light on the discursive power of gendered whiteness during its 19th-century invention. It is important to illuminate and interrogate this self-constructed discourse of white women's selflessness and self-proclaimed heroism for several reasons: primarily, it demonstrates the precise moment in time during which white womanhood became conflated with innocent heroism (although historically it has been always been symbolic of innocence); secondly, paying attention to white missionary women's voices makes visible the intersection of the putting into discourse the imagined benevolent teacher/savior role of white women with the larger, presumably masculine project of the US Global Empire and white supremacy; thirdly, because it demonstrates a certain type of white woman drawn to teaching, and the discourse around teaching as a calling, from the beginning of formalized schooling and continuing to the present. Further, it is particularly important and relevant that we read missionary women's words through a critical lens, as they (the women and their writing) were far more influential in the US settler colonial project and in the furthering of a discursive benevolent whiteness than published history has previously acknowledged. Missionaries were required to keep extensive written records in the form of letters (to family, funders, and church) and private journals. Many additionally hand-copied their letters home into a bound journal prior to mailing. These writings were widely read by contemporaries during the 19th century, and many were later published into what now serves as the main written record of this period in US educational and colonial expansion, thus constructing the truth of the era and the trope for the future. As such, it is important to (re)read these writings through a lens of both settler colonialism and women of color feminism – building on Arvin, Tuck, and Morril (2013) a gendering of settler colonialism as a structure and process – to adjust the dominant discourse on our collective conception of the roles of white women in the US settler colonial project and in schooling children of color throughout history to the present.

On "Tender Violence" and Its Genealogical Significance

Titling this book "Tender Violence" is an aesthetic choice, a critique of its missionary origins, and a continuation of genealogical connection. The precision and aptness of the phrase are, of course, due to its initial utterance by Hampton Institute founder General Samuel Chapman Armstrong describing his pedagogical method for assimilating into whiteness and capitalist productivity his Native American and formerly enslaved African students. Armstrong described his methods as a "tender, judicious and patient, yet vigorously educational system," a system of "tender violence" to "rouse" darker races from innate ignorance and deficiency of character (Armstrong, 1884, p. 213; Engs, 1979, cited in Wexler, 2000, p. 108), so they might be "cleaned and tamed by a simple process" also called "the Hampton Method" (S. C. Armstrong cited in Lindsey, 1995, p. 112). What on the surface appear to be starkly different concerns – the history of colonial schooling in Hawai'i and the systematized anti-Blackness in US schools – through Armstrong become genealogically connected: their threads of similarity and relationality woven together by the notion of tender violence. The revelation that Armstrong and his family had been responsible for spreading this pedagogical violence across generations, oceans, and the US continent should not be ignored. As I describe in more detail in Chapter 3, when discussing Hampton, Armstrong credited his missionary parents' methods for Christianizing Kanaka Maoli as inspirational for his own designs for Black and Native American students. The "problem" of what to do with "darker races" in the United States was in his mind "worked out in the Hawaiian Islands," later perfected at Hampton, and then brought across the continent to subdue and Americanize Indigenous peoples by former Hampton teachers like Elaine Goodale Eastman (see Chapter 4). Thus, tender violence in its original utterance is revealed to have traveled the global mission trails through schooling, with the intention to control and assimilate rather than educate and enlighten the non-white masses.

Yet, the tender violence goes far deeper than the obvious similarities in missionary pedagogical strategies used to subdue both Black and Indigenous peoples through schooling. Evolved iterations of tender violence as paternalism persisted throughout history and remain ever-present in contemporary schools. We can see evidence of its pedagogical immortality not only in notions behind "tough-love-for-your-own-good" disciplinary policies, but also in the way 19th-century manual and domestic education for the masses has been replaced by a myopic insistence on "coding for all," herding a generation of structurally oppressed students into an unending stream of workers, but not thinkers or designers, in the brave new tech world.[5] Thus, Armstrong's tender violence once intended to prepare one century's citizenry for assimilation and work to uphold capitalism and global conquest simply reinvents itself with each passing generation.

In addition to the intergenerational violence of Armstrong's educational model, I am intrigued by the way the phrase itself has circulated and been taken up and critiqued in recent years. I first came across his term "tender violence" quoted in a dissertation talk given by a classmate, Funie Hsu, who drew important connections between Armstrong's tender violence and the "coloniality of English" taught by US military officers as the primary teachers in 19th-century schools in the Philippines (see Hsu, 2013 for the dissertation). Soon after, in her 2014 article "Domesticating Hawaiians: Kamehameha Schools and the 'Tender Violence' of Marriage," Kanaka 'Ōiwi scholar Noelani Goodyear-Ka'ōpua beautifully dissected the multiple meanings of "tender" to add nuance and depth to our understanding of the school-based violence enacted by Armstrong and his successors across time and distance. Goodyear-Kaʻōpua traces the violent consequences of the Kamehameha Schools falling under "exclusive haole control" as not only tender in the original sense of being lovingly paternalistic, but also as constructing Kanaka as feminized (tender as soft, malleable, childlike), as well as positioning us economically and socially as the tender "permanently coupled as a productive force" on the steam train of white supremacy and plantation capitalism through the school's focus on manual and domestic education.

Finally, in tracing the uptake of "tender violence" reimagined as an analytical tool, all roads lead back to Laura Wexler's 2001 book on American women photojournalists at the turn of the 20th century, *Tender Violence: Domestic Visions in an Age of US Imperialism*. In her introduction Wexler states, "By focusing on the strengths and limitations of gender as an instrumental force in the field of vision, I hope to provide a sharper, more politically nuanced view of what it meant to the women" in the past as photojournalists and "what it still might mean to us" (p. 14). I scribbled in the margins, "Yes! This is exactly what I'm trying to do with teachers/schools!" Coming across this book, cited in both Hsu's and Goodyear-Kaʻōpua's work, was like finding a kindred intellectual spirit, an unintentional interlocutor confirming my ideas were not as outlandish as the extant scholarship on 19th-century womanhood would have us believe. I owe a huge debt of gratitude to Wexler for her analysis of white middle-class women's power historically hidden behind a discourse of innocence and powerlessness under patriarchy. Wexler analyzed the images created and circulated by white women photojournalists in the 20th century, noting how they upheld US empire through what she terms the "averted gaze" of domestic sentiment used to "normalize and inscribe raced and classed relations of dominance" and "the innocent eye" that "designated a deeply problematic practice of representation" (2000, p. 6) which together worked to evoke an imagined gendered intimacy. Her analysis resonates with how I understand the letter and diaries written and circulated by white women educators in the 19th century, which similarly evoke an artificial gendered intimacy with the targets of colonization – Indigenous, Black, and Other-presumed-savage peoples. I discovered her book at the most serendipitous moment in my own intellectual journey; the affirmation it provided for my own nascent analysis of white womanhood was precisely what I needed to continue with the project.

Overview of the Chapters in This Book

In Chapter 1, "(En)Gendering Whiteness: Toward a Theory of Benevolent Whiteness," I discuss the importance of using the 19th century as a temporal frame and introduce the idea of white women's confessional literature (diaries, letters, etc.) as iterative violence, contemplating the politics and potential limitations of my choice to center white women's voices in this way. I also build on Foucault (1977), Brodhead (1988), and Jacobs (2005) to set forth my theorization of "benevolent whiteness," birthed by the Victorian "Cult of True Womanhood" (Welter, 1966) and incubated in the newly feminized profession of teaching. I develop and extend extant theories to demonstrate the importance of making visible the permanence of a trope of heroic maternal labor that relies on "benevolent whiteness" in education. To do so, I offer a brief historical explanation for the conflation of mothering and teaching as women's godly work, which I propose as a discursively constructed concept that persists to the present day, and which is an important and unrecognized foundation that undergirds race- and gender-based inequities in school discipline trends. I also suggest connections between benevolent whiteness as an answer to a holy calling, and its specific and intentional role in furthering of the US white nation-state. Looking forward, the chapter closes with a framework for viewing each subsequent chapter and the book as a whole through a lens of Black and Indigenous "futurity, futurisms, and resurgence" as a means to re-envision and put into practice decolonial future-making through educational endeavors (Goodyear-Ka'ōpua, 2018).

Chapter 2, "Woman on a Mission: Lucy Goodale Thurston," is framed within the social and political contexts of the early 19th century (beginning in 1820). This chapter tells the story of the feminine arm of empire as flexed by women of the American Board of Commissioners for Foreign Missions (ABCFM), with a focus on the life and works of missionary Lucy Goodale Thurston. In considering the role of white womanhood in general, and that of Lucy Thurston specifically, this chapter asks how we can begin to see the discursive construction of a benevolent whiteness – a cult of true womanhood – that characterizes itself as wholly benevolent, innocent, and salvation-oriented, and what remnants of this are evident in contemporary narratives about schooling and saving students of color. Lucy's story gives us insight into the impetus behind white women teaching Indigenous children (and adults, who were perceived as children) in the 19th century, and in a more general way into the minds of women regardless of era who are "called" into teaching with hopes of saving Black and Brown children from themselves and their families. Further, the work of Lucy and her contemporaries as evidenced by their own diaries and subsequent histories and biographies makes clear the conflation of evangelicalism with teaching: schools functioned as a tool for spreading Christianity to "heathen" populations while simultaneously furthering US white middle-class values of capitalism and imperial domination in the name of enlightenment. These qualities born alongside organized schooling are deeply embedded in the role of the female teacher, amalgamated to a point where they cannot be individuated or decoupled from the white female teacher's identity without explicit work and intention. The chapter concludes by drawing parallels between the missionary roots and contemporary embodiment of benevolent whiteness in US schools, challenging would-be educators, veteran teachers, school leaders, and others to evaluate their desires for and commitments to "saving" historically oppressed students, and to sit with the reality of their participation within the systems of reproductive white supremacy. Chapter 3, "The Invasion of Light and Love: Laura Matilda Town," focuses on the US postwar South, specifically the Sea Islands off the coast of Georgia and South Carolina. It begins with the US political and social context at the time, starting with the Civil War and through Reconstruction. After the Civil War and in response to Black emancipation, a massive influx of white northern teachers arrived in the south. The American Missionary Association (AMA) sent nearly 80% of all northern teachers in postwar Georgia, following the methods and intentions previously set in Hawai'i, in Indian Country, and in other colonial outposts around the globe. All AMA teachers were missionaries whose roles included equal focus on religious conversion as well as education with a shared goal of unifying the United States under the tenets of Protestantism and capitalism (Jones, 1980, p. 5). In the Sea Islands, however, the missionary educational force was requested by the US military and supported by the federal government. Named the Port Royal Experiment, this mission was an experiment in exercising control over the abandoned (but not yet freed) Black population through schooling and a protestant work ethic rather than through the more overt violence of slavery. This chapter further develops the connections between anti-Indigeneity and anti-Blackness as manifested through benevolent whiteness and the US imperialist project, with a specific focus on the deployment of white women teachers as the ideological arm of anti-Blackness – the counterpart to the more recognizably violent white male military troops. This chapter argues that an understanding of the genealogy of schooling in the United States, and a desire to imagine its decolonized futures, require a nuanced understanding of the relationships between settler colonialism and anti-Blackness and the roles schools and teachers have played in supporting those structures. It also makes visible in the ruptures and erasures how Black and Indigenous communities have historically and contemporarily created spaces of resistance and solidarity. Toward this end, educational scholars, teachers, school leaders, and community members of color along with white accomplices are compelled and positioned to break free from the violent trappings of settler colonialism and anti-Blackness and bring forth multiple new educational futurities.

Chapter 4, "Sister to the Sioux: Elaine Goodale Eastman," turns toward the role of white womanhood and benevolent whiteness as constructed in Native American Indian boarding schools. This chapter is again framed within the social and political contexts of the time, tracing the circuit of benevolent whiteness as it travels back to its roots, often by way of missionary descendants who took what they learned in Hawai'i and applied it unilaterally toward the education of Indigenous peoples (and emancipated Black people) on the continent. As in the previous chapter, I ask readers to consider how we can view 19th-century women's diaries and journals – their "truths" – through a lens that clarifies the history of teaching and schools as sites of settler colonialism, its related violence, and the gendered power dynamics traditionally normalized or made invisible by the very women in power. This complicates the narrative that white women in the 19th century were entirely without agency and were themselves only victims of patriarchy and thus *unwilling* participants in the violence required for US imperial expansion. Tracing and analyzing the repeated recitations of love and benevolence found in these women's letters and diaries, this chapter asks readers to consider what it means when "good intentions" end up with malevolent results, and, more importantly, why we insist collectively that good intentions excuse negative outcomes. How can we decouple "good intentions" from the structural, ideological, physical, and material violence that so often results from benevolent whiteness and its loving intentions? Who determines what intentions are good in the first place? After all, colonialism was benevolent in the eyes of the colonizer state, as were missions in the minds of missionaries, regardless of their genocidal effects on Indigenous peoples, colonized tribal nations, and enslaved Africans. Again, this chapter closes by connecting schooling's deep missionary roots to their contemporary overgrowth in US schools. Through weaving these connections, I ask readers to complicate their understandings of "good intentions" and teaching as an act of love, to consider that their desires to serve and "save" historically oppressed students oftentimes reinforce and reproduce violent white supremacy.

Finally, Chapter 5, "A Woman's Work Is Never Done: Benevolent Whiteness in 'Post-Racial' America," considers the implications of this study, particularly in relation to training a new generation of teachers that continues to be predominantly white and female. In this era that, until recently, was lauded as "post-racial," benevolent whiteness continues to function, although arguably in a mutated form, in contemporary women's writings as well as through "alternative" teaching programs like Teach For America. White womanhood continues to operate through hidden wages of whiteness, hidden under its cloak of invisible normativity, innocence, and perpetual victimhood under patriarchy. The collective national discourse on teaching and teachers in "underserved" or "urban" schools remains focused on inherent benevolence and heroism, a chorus perpetually singing the praises of those who dare to do this "thankless" and seemingly impossibly work for the betterment of the nation. Benevolent whiteness in our schools persists, with little interrogation of the good intentions that result in malevolent outcomes. This chapter concludes the book by asking us to consider how and why benevolent whiteness persists, particularly in our schools. How has it changed over time to meet the needs of the white supremacy, and how much of it is simply residual conditioning, remnants of a 19th-century trope that continues to function to the detriment of students of color? Regardless of whether teachers' uptake of benevolent whiteness is conscious or subconscious (or anywhere in between), the important question moving forward is how can benevolent whiteness be located and dislocated in contemporary classrooms and teacher preparation programs? Toward that end, the book concludes with an imperative that any real possibilities for decolonial schooling must be envisioned through the interrelated lenses of Black and Indigenous futurity.

Notes

1 Regarding the capitalization of "Black" throughout this book, I am following Dumas (2016) who explains this choice as follows: "In my work, I have decided to capitalize Black when referencing Black people, organizations, and cultural products. Here, Black is understood as a self determined name of a racialized social group that shares a specific set of histories, cultural processes, and imagined and performed kinships. White is not capitalized in my work because it is nothing but a social construct, and does not describe a group with a sense of common experiences or kinship outside of acts of colonization and terror. Thus, white is employed almost solely as a negation of others – it is, as David Roediger (1994) insisted, *nothing but* false and oppressive."

2 The term "discipline gap" was first introduced by Gregory and Mosely in their 2004 article "The Discipline Gap: Teachers' Views on the Over-representation of African American Students in the Discipline System." *Equity & Excellence in Education*, 37(1), 18–30. The discipline gap, named after the more widely discussed "achievement gap" between Black students and their white and Asian peers, refers to the over-representation of Black students in disciplinary referrals.

3 *Waiting for Superman* (2010), *Dangerous Minds* (1995, starring Pfeiffer), and *Freedom Writers* (2007, starring Swank) are all contemporary narratives focused on "heroic" teachers and students of color in need of "saving."

4 Here, I employ the term "genealogy" as described by Foucault in a 1983 interview with Paul Rabinow and Herbert Dreyfus as having three possible domains. I specifically focus on the second possible domain, "a historical ontology of ourselves in relation to a field of power through which we constitute ourselves as subjects acting on others" (Foucault and Rabinow, 1984, p. 351).

5 For an excellent analysis of this topic, see Vossoughi, S., & Vakil, S. (2018). Toward what ends? A critical analysis of militarism, equity, and STEM education. In *Education at War* (pp. 117–140), and Vakil, S., & Ayers, R. (2019). The racial politics of STEM education in the USA: Interrogations and explorations. *Race Ethnicity and Education*, 22(4), 449–458.

References

Armstrong, S. C. (1884). *Lessons from the Hawaiian Islands*. Hampton, VA: Publisher not identified.

Arvin, M., Tuck, E., & Morrill, A. (2013). Decolonizing feminism: Challenging connections between settler colonialism and heteropatriarchy. *Feminist Formations*, 25(1), 8–34.

Brodhead, R. H. (1988). Sparing the rod: Discipline and fiction in antebellum America. *Representations*, 21, 67–96.

Collins, P. H. (2002). *Black feminist thought: Knowledge, consciousness, and the politics of empowerment*. New York, NY: Routledge.

Crenshaw, K. (1991). Mapping the margins: Intersectionality, identity politics, and violence against women of color. *Stanford Law Review*, 43, 1241–1299.

Dumas, M. J. (2016). Against the dark: Antiblackness in education policy and discourse. *Theory Into Practice*, 55(1), 11–19.

Engs, R. F. (1979). *Freedom's first generation: Black Hampton, Virginia, 1861–1890* (p. 195). Philadelphia: University of Pennsylvania Press.

Foucault, M. (1977). *Discipline and punish: The birth of the prison.* New York, NY: Vintage Books.

Foucault, M., & Rabinow, P. (1984). *The Foucault reader.* New York, NY: Pantheon Books.

Goodyear-Kaʻōpua, N. (2014). Domesticating Hawaiians: Kamehameha schools and the "tender violence" of marriage. In B. J. Child (Ed.), *Indian subjects: Hemispheric perspectives on the history of indigenous education* (pp. 16–47). Edited by Brenda J. Child & Brian Klopotek. First edition. School for Advanced Research Press.

Goodyear-Kaʻōpua, N. (2018). Indigenous oceanic futures: Challenging settler colonialisms and militarization. In L. Tuhiwai Smith, E. Tuck & K. W. Yang (Eds.), *Indigenous and decolonizing studies in education* (pp. 82–102). Abingdon: Routledge.

Gregory, A., & Mosely, P. M. (2004). The discipline gap: Teachers' views on the over-representation of African American students in the discipline system. *Equity & Excellence in Education, 37*(1), 18–30.

Guggenheim, D. (Director). (2010). *Waiting for "Superman."* Hollywood, CA: [Film]. Paramount Pictures.

Hsu, F. (2013). *Colonial articulations: English instruction and the 'benevolence' of U.S. overseas expansion in the Philippines, 1898–1916* (Order No. 3593854). Berkeley: University of California. Available from Ethnic NewsWatch. (1441349845).

Jacobs, M. D. (2005). Maternal colonialism: White women and indigenous child removal in the American West and Australia, 1880–1940. *Western Historical Quarterly, 36*(4), 453–476. doi:10.2307/25443236.

Jacobs, M. D. (2009). *White mother to a dark race: Settler colonialism, maternalism, and the removal of indigenous children in the American west and Australia, 1880–1940.* Lincoln: University of Nebraska Press.

Jones, J. (1980). *Soldiers of light and love: Northern teachers and Georgia blacks, 1865–1873.* Chapel Hill, NC: University of North Carolina press.

Kameʻeleihiwa, L. (1992). *Native lands and Foreign desires: Pehea lā e pono ai?* Honolulu: Bishop Museum Press.

Kauanui, J. K. (2018). *Paradoxes of Hawaiian sovereignty.* Durham, NC: Duke University Press.

Kipling, R. (1899). *The white man's burden: A poem.* New York, NY: Doubleday and McClure Co.

LaGravenese, R. (Director). (2007). *Freedom writers.* Hollywood, LA: [Film]. MTV Films.

Leonardo, Z. (2009). *Race, whiteness, and education.* New York, NY: Routledge.

Lindsey, D. F. (1995). *Indians at Hampton Institute, 1877–1923.* Urbana: University of Illinois Press.

Moreton-Robinson, A. (2021). *Talkin' up to the white woman: Indigenous women and feminism.* Minneapolis: University of Minnesota Press.

Perkins, U. (2019). Moʻokūʻauhau and Mana. In N. Wilson-Hokowhitu (Ed.). *The past before us: Moʻokūʻauhau as methodology.* (pp. 69–79). Honolulu: University of Hawaii Press.

Roediger, D. (1994). *Toward the abolition of whiteness.* New York, NY: Verso.

Roediger, D. (1999). *The wages of whiteness: Race and the making of the American working class.* New York, NY: Verso.

Sandoval, C. (2000). *Methodology of the oppressed.* Minneapolis: University of Minnesota Press.

Smith, J. (Director). (1995). *Dangerous minds.* USA: [Film]. Hollywood Pictures.

Vakil, S., & Ayers, R. (2019). The racial politics of STEM education in the USA: Interrogations and explorations. *Race Ethnicity and Education, 22*(4), 449–458.

Vossoughi, S., & Vakil, S. (2018). Toward what ends? A critical analysis of militarism, equity, and STEM education In Arshad Imtiaz Ali & Tracy Lachica Buenavista (Ed.). *Education at War* (pp. 117–140). New York, NY: Fordham University Press.

Welter, B. (1966). The cult of true womanhood: 1820–1860. *American Quarterly, 18*(2), 151–174.

Wexler, L. (2000). *Tender violence: Domestic visions in an age of U.S. imperialism.* Chapel Hill: University of North Carolina Press.

1

(EN)GENDERING WHITENESS

Toward a Theory of Benevolent Whiteness

One might rightfully argue that the reality of the United States in the 21st century is not that of the 19th century, the former being a system of mature capitalism while the latter was an era of colonial capitalist expansion of empire; yet both seemingly different experiences/moments continue to serve the same hidden ends: capitalist white supremacy. This book argues that benevolent whiteness, as the feminized arm of empire, and what is more easily legible as overt white supremacy, are bolstered through the discourse of loving maternalism and the corporeal and ideological disciplining of Black and Brown bodies through schooling. Through this analysis, I explain how the collective acceptance of and participation in the discursive construction of heroic white womanhood has been invisibly and normatively influential, in various temporal and geographic locations, in the discursive underpinnings of US educational and disciplinary practice for nearly 200 years. Toward that end, this book provides a critical link between the past and the present and re-centers and refocuses on whiteness as an ideology and racial discourse (Leonardo, 2002) rather than as a static identity category. In doing so, I provide an opening for teachers and researchers to consider multiple and overlapping ways that over-disciplining students of color, a task largely performed by white females in an institution haunted by the specter of an imagined benevolent whiteness, can be understood as expressions of contemporary "colonial anxieties" (Stoler, 2003) and as a consequence of our settler colonial past and present.

Background on "The Cult of White Womanhood"

> The empire of the woman is an empire of softness … her commands are caresses, her menaces are tears.
>
> – Jean-Jacques Rousseau (1768)

DOI: 10.4324/9781003201809-2

By the mid-19th century, white womanhood gained a new authoritative foothold in the United States. Already held in the highest regard, mid-century white women (minus the "fallen" – poor, prostitutes, recent immigrants) were considered inherently holy and pious, enshrined as the mothers of the nation and thus the obvious protectors of the family's and the nation's moral compasses. Defined by what is now termed the "Cult of True Womanhood" (as described by historian Barbara Welter, 1966), white women saw themselves as "a new and holy army, a national 'army of women'" meant to solidify white statehood through healing the fissure between the postwar North and South (Blum, 2005, p. 179).

Although women's "proper" domain was once confined to the spaces of home and family, changes in the 19th-century economy opened a new door for white women: that of the schoolhouse. The schoolhouse, at this moment, became newly imagined as feminized – as an extension of the space of the domestic, a site of moral as well as practical education. Prior to this shift, young white men made up the majority of the nation's teachers, a workforce seen as a temporary holding ground for those preparing for other professions (Apple, 1985; Strober & Lanford, 1986; Clifford, 1989; Rury, 1989). Two major changes contributed to a mass exodus of men from the primary school classrooms: (1) a change in available work, from home-based skilled labor to work outside of the home in factories and other newly expanding professions, and (2) as the public schooling movement grew compulsory and more bureaucratic, men moved into the higher-paying and more powerful and respectable positions of management and administration (Apple, 1985; Strober & Lanford, 1986). Thus, by the mid-19th century, young, single white women staffed classrooms across the country in unprecedented numbers, rapidly constituting the majority of the nation's teachers (Clifford, 1989; Rury, 1989; Sedlak & Schlossman, 1986), a majority they continue to hold over a century and a half later. Women's roles as mothering disciplinarians both at home and at school were created simultaneously and were conflated to include a primary focus on teaching morality and discipline through women's "inherent talents" of mothering, loving, and instilling in students a desire to obey and thus maintaining their surrogate mothers' affections.

At the same time teaching became feminized, the United States was in the midst of its greatest period of colonial expansion, with the ideological arm of the empire belonging to missionary teachers. In the latter half of the 19th century, the number of missionaries from the Presbyterian Church alone rose from fewer than 100 to more than 10,000 across the globe (Blum, 2005). In this context, white women's roles expanded from serving as vanguards of morality for their own and the nation's white children, to stepping in as the moral vanguards for all nonwhite children and their parents within the United States and its occupied territories (Adams, 1995) as well as for those white children whose birth and status put them outside of the middle-class moral sphere of their teachers. It is in this moment that the white woman's burden was discursively cemented in the nation's collective psyche.

It is this culturally specific, temporally located invention of sacred white mother as guardian and vanguard of whiteness that I am arguing has persisted beyond its 19th-century Protestant roots, resulting in a colonial schoolhouse model that has not changed significantly over time, and neither has its related imagination of the proper student subject nor the role of the surrogate mother/teacher. Relatedly, the racist and colonialist ideological and practical roots that undergird the myth of the teacher as maternal moral stand-in structurally upholds and requires myths of a dangerous and untutored "other" that threatens a mythic, fragile, maternal whiteness.

The 19th Century as Temporal Frame

This book is temporally situated amid the United States' greatest period of colonial capitalist expansion, which necessarily coincided with the organization and systematization of public schooling as an ideological state apparatus (Althusser, 1971). Beginning with the first group of missionaries to the Kingdom of Hawai'i in 1820, the book traces the circuitry of benevolent whiteness and settler colonialism as they travel both discursively and literally, following the descendants of the first Hawai'i missionaries back to North America as teachers and "reformers" of education for Indigenous tribes and newly freed Black citizens of the postwar South.

The 19th century's systemization of schooling tends to be remembered with a symbolically significant false nostalgia as the era during which education was freely provided for all, with the benevolent intent of creating equality and opportunity as its sole purpose. This is the false memory of a leveled playing field which never was; a misremembering of a state system meant to peacefully welcome all peoples to climb into the great melting pot of "America." Framing this book within this period, with a focus on how white women in particular imagined themselves as heroes within and outside of the violence of settler colonialism, is important for several reasons: primarily, it dispels the falsehood that there ever existed a time during which schools were disentangled from white supremacy. Secondly, situating each chapter within the social and political happenings of the 19th century allows for a more complex, nuanced understanding of the otherwise seemingly benign and benevolent acts carried out by "educational reformers" over the past two centuries. This orientation engenders a critical understand of the insidious nature of white supremacy as it is embedded in ostensibly innocuous structures (schools, missionary organizations, the women's rights movement, and reform movements in general) and as it works to further US imperial expansion. Finally, understanding the gendering of whiteness and white supremacy through a genealogical framework makes visible precisely how women accepted "wages of whiteness" (Roediger, 1999) attaining individual power and freedom in exchange for their nurturing and upholding of white supremacy through settler colonialism. Despite the temporal framing of this book within the 19th century, it is important to clarify that although what is more commonsensically understood as colonialism defined much of the empirical desire of the United States at this time, this book focuses on *settler colonialism* as an entirely different structure that continues to exist today. Patrick Wolfe (1999) is perhaps the most cited scholar of settler colonialism, famous for stating that settler colonialism "is both as complex social formation and as continuity through time … a structure rather than an event." As defined by Cavanagh and Veracini (2013),

> Settler colonialism is a global and transnational phenomenon, and as much a thing of the past as a thing of the present. There is no such thing as neo-settler colonialism or post-settler colonialism because settler colonialism is a resilient formation that rarely ends.… And settler colonialism is not colonialism: settlers want Indigenous people to vanish (but can make use of their labour before they are made to disappear).

Women's Confessional Literature as Iterative Violence

In this book, I analyze white women's confessional literature (diaries, memoirs, letters) as an archive to make visible the discursive power of gendered whiteness as it was invented in the 19th century. It is important to illuminate and interrogate this self-constructed discourse of white women's selflessness and self-proclaimed heroism for several reasons: primarily, it demonstrates the precise moment in time during which white womanhood became conflated with innocent heroism (although historically it has been always been symbolic of innocence); secondly, paying attention to white missionary women's voices makes visible the intersection between the discourse of the imagined benevolent teacher/savior role of white women and the larger, presumably masculine project of the United States' Global Empire and white supremacy; thirdly, because it demonstrates a certain type of white woman drawn to teaching, and the discourse around teaching as a calling, from the beginning of formalized schooling and continuing to the present. Further, it is highly important and relevant that we read missionary women's words through a critical lens,[1] as they (both the women and their writing) were far more influential in the US settler colonial project and in furthering discursive "benevolent whiteness" than published history has previously acknowledged.

Missionary women (and men) were required to keep extensive written records in the form of letters (to family, funders, and church) and private journals. Many additionally hand-copied their letters home into a bound journal prior to mailing. These writings were widely read by contemporaries during the 19th century, and many were later published into what now serves as the main written record of this period in US educational and colonial expansion.

As such, it is important to critically (re-)read these writings to adjust the dominant discourse on our collective conception of the roles of white women in the US settler colonial project and in schooling children of color throughout history to the present.

Disciplinary Intimacy and the Feminization of Teaching

When the rod gets laid aside in nineteenth-century domesticity, it is because it is no longer needed in the disciplinary arsenal, having been replaced by psychological weapons with new orders of coercive power.

(Brodhead, 1988, p. 87)

According to Foucault in *Discipline and Punish*, the "historical period" of punishment serves as the transition period between the sovereign torture state and the modern disciplinary state. Foucault discusses, crucially, the figure of the delinquent ("controlled legality," 1977, p. 279), distinguished from the offender. The figure of the delinquent is one who is hopelessly recidivist due to his own moral failings. Paradoxically, the prison (and the school system) produces the "delinquent," requiring the delinquent in order to survive and retain purpose. The delinquent is the degenerate other of normalcy, and thus, the enemy of the people. The delinquent exists to make the prison necessary. This idea of the requisite delinquent is both resulting from, and required for, benevolent whiteness.

Brodhead (1988) builds on Foucault's theories to propose a theory of "disciplinary intimacy" made commonsensical[2] through a combination of 19th-century parenting manuals and popular fiction, and as a means of distancing the "respectable" progressives of the North from corporal punishment as slavery's "ultimate referent" (p. 68). In antebellum decades, northerners' expressions of outrage against whipping (in any site of punishment) were a veritable Foucauldian "cry from the heart" that "began stigmatizing physical punishment in early modernity as an outrage to 'humanity.'" In response, northern educational reformers advocated for "less visible but more persuasive, less 'cruel' but more deeply controlling" technologies of social regulation (p. 69). As such, disciplinary intimacy, or "discipline through love," is heralded as both creating and created by the nation's nascent middle class.

Following Foucault, Brodhead cites a change in disciplinary practice from visible, external acts (here, the whipping of the slave) as symbolic of the public impression upon the body via the marks of the transgressor's sins and the corrective power of authority, toward the "less visible but more persuasive, less 'cruel' but more deeply controlling" technologies of social regulation (p. 69). Foucault explains how disciplinary power transitions from the power of the sovereign, which exists in the body of the king but is not confined therein, to a power that is less visible and in fact invisible – as in the panopticon. Here, power becomes a technology: something that is not held, but simply functions. Disciplinary power functions through the idea of the *surveiller:* the unseen but all-seeing observer at the center of the panopticon who can be anyone or no one. Foucault's idea is based on Bentham's panopticon, a design intended to be an ideal prison which was never actualized, though its design has been applied to many contemporary structures, including schools. In Bentham's panoptic design, "power should be visible and unverifiable" (Foucault, 1977, p. 201), resulting in an inmate population that acts as its own guard, functioning under the assumption that they could, at any time, be under surveillance. Foucault's theorization suggests that panopticism results in self-monitoring and self-regulation, amplifying power through internalization of rules and normalization of subjects (p. 206).

Conversely, Brodhead describes a changing disciplinary power in the 19th century as "against both these formulations": disciplinary power as love (disciplinary intimacy) resides *in* the female authority figure, and it also becomes "dissolved into their very personal pretense" (Brodhead, 1988, p. 71), resulting in the personification of authority/power rather than an understanding of authority as a transpersonal right. Therefore, authority figures (in this case, female teachers) represent power symbolically while they also hold power literally and functionally. This is important to keep in mind, as teachers often attempt to absolve themselves of agency in the formal punishing of students, citing what they see as a problematic lack of power in their roles and blaming suspensions and other punishments on school administrators with whom the proverbial buck officially stops. Brodhead's theorization of female authoritative power suggests that teachers' discursive self-positioning as disempowered subjects of a larger system is not only harmful but also categorically untrue.

The birth of disciplinary intimacy resulted not only from the North's rejection of slavery and its referents, but also from an important transition in gendered family dynamics which can be seen as both necessary for, and the result of, the developing middle class: mothers as authority figures. The new middle class distanced itself from the poor and the past via the emphasis on the new role of the father who worked outside of the home, and mothers whose sole responsibility was to safeguard the morals of her children, and thus the nation, through her modeling and teaching of proper behavior. In support of this effort, an overabundance of books and pamphlets were published to advise women on using their inherent feminine powers (manipulative feelings of love) to embed a "deep burial of morality" (Brodhead, 1988, p. 146) into their children "aiming toward inward colonialism" (p. 147). Books on child rearing[3] instructed mothers in the humanization of authority as a replacement for the harsher (masculine) scolding and physical punishment of the father. Following this method, as a successful disciplinarian, a mother would punish with a look rather than a lash, having enveloped her charges within an intense emotional bond of love, guilt, and obligation.

The role of mother as authority through love coincided with the compulsory public school movement, with a conflation of teaching and mothering "traced to a mixture of 19th-century prescriptions for middle-class mothers and theorizing by Froebel and other reformers about what is natural mothering and how it can be realized in the classroom" (Acker, 1995, p. 121). The middle-class home, in fact, necessitated a nationwide public school system as a site for the extension of middle-class values enforced via disciplinary intimacy. Horace Mann (cited in Broadhead), in his prolific writings, represented the common school as "disciplinary intimacy's second home" (p. 148), and schoolteachers as surrogate mothers to ill-bred children (p. 149). This historical nexus continues to shape dangerously masked notions that position students of color as delinquents to be saved, yet always already lost by white teacher-saviors.

As I have illustrated generally, the "feminization of teaching" began in the mid-1800s and was all but completed by the turn of the century. This shift – both in labor force and in the perception of the work itself – occurred across geographic locations. While I have outlined the larger cultural changes that informed this shift, its nature was also affected by a variety of contributing factors. The teaching profession first, for example, became female-dominated in places where schooling was organized and formalized, beginning with New England, the Mid-Atlantic, the Midwest, and large urban areas. In rural and pre-formalized areas, teaching remained, for a longer time, a path toward motherhood and marriage for women, and a stepping-stone toward a more lucrative occupation for men who had fewer options than their urban counterparts (Rury, 1989; Strober & Lanford, 1986). The shift in teachers' backgrounds from rural white men toward middle-class white women across the country was finally due to both changes in the economy and changes in the educational system itself – in the systemizing of education (Apple, 1985).

Scholars generally agree upon four main causes for the shift toward teaching as "women's work" (notwithstanding the larger umbrella cause of the cult of true womanhood): (1) cost – women could be hired for pennies on the dollar compared to equally (or less) qualified men; (2) women were seen as inherently better with younger children, and naturally inclined to impart morality and caring to their young charges; (3) the formalization of teaching and schooling was designed for female teachers, specifically the length of the school year; as the lengthened school year precluded men from engaging in full time agricultural work while using teaching as a source of "off season" extra income, it led to an increase in demand for female teachers and a decrease in supply for male teachers; (4) women were seen as easily controlled and bureaucratized, and thus a more desirable work force controlled by men in central administrative positions (Apple, 1985; Grumet, 1988; Montgomery, 2009; Rury, 1989; Strober & Lanford, 1986). Considering both the larger ideological shift that "sanctioned" teaching as "proper" work and these more specific causes, what we know for sure is that women moved into teaching when and where there were few educated men willing to teach and, therefore, by the latter half of the 19th century, the profession was overwhelmingly female.

The Great White Mother as the Educative Arm of Empire

As I intimated earlier, this female army of teachers was not simply charged with educating United States' children, but with extending its reach abroad. Nineteenth-century constructions of gender dictated that white women's inherent obligations were to spend their lives caring for (instilling moral values in) their families or teaching school (instilling moral values in other people's children) – each a different arm of the same beast intended to protect the white republic. Margaret Jacobs (2005, 2009) explores this too-often ignored significance of gender in the colonial project via her theorization of the "Great White Mother" trope. The "Great White Mother" recalls the Cult of True Womanhood and refers to white women as active agents of the state, as moral arbiters at home and abroad, in the "post-frontier phase of internal colonialism." Like disciplinary intimacy I discussed above, this tool of the state is one that operates through less visibly violent although no less dangerous mechanisms than masculine colonial power.

Unlike the more recognizably violent phases of colonialism, the murder and displacement of Indigenous peoples for the purpose of furthering US manifest destiny, internal (maternal) colonialism consists of women's work focused on the management of Indigenous women's bodies and homes (including their children). The missionary woman's task was and still is to attempt to sever children's ties between family and culture, to educate and indoctrinate them into a narrowly defined, white, middle-class Protestant ideal. Jacobs (2005, 2009) problematizes the self-appointed savior role of 19th-century white women by exploring their paradoxical stance as supposed advocates for Indigenous women's rights while simultaneously advocating for the state sanctioned removal of Indigenous children from their "unfit" homes. Jacobs' work makes clear that white women were not merely victims of a white supremacist patriarchy, but that they indeed were active agents of the colonial process who took advantage of their prescribed roles as "sacred nurturers" to promote their agenda within the workings of a patriarchal state. That is, elevating white womanhood, and thus potentially reacting to and railing against women's marginalized status, required (and continues to require) the pathologizing of nonwhite womanhood. White missionary women worked the system to their advantage and advancement as key participants in the systematic dehumanization of nonwhite peoples, gaining advantage and power from their active enforcement of a system that empowered and ennobled them (Jacobs, 2005, p. 456).

The failure to name and interrogate white women as more than just "innocent bystanders to colonial conquest" leaves a chasm in the history of the United States and unduly reiterates the belief in the frontier experience as central to the contemporary American character, including democracy and materialism; it names the cause as the effect while neither holding accountable nor making visible the true basis of American character as white supremacist, patriarchal, and colonialist. Ignoring white women's agency within the "army of whiteness" (Leonardo & Boas, 2013) represses the ways in which white women discursively positioned themselves as heroically doing "God's work" through love and salvation, all the while publicly touting their beloved status among nonwhite mothers who happily handed over their children (Brodhead, 1988; Coloma, 2012; Jacobs, 2005). The erasure of this history means that its repercussions remain invisible – not only in our educational system but in similar formulations in NGOSs, "voluntourism," and countless "white savior" female narratives.

It is this persona as a beloved mother-substitute, devoid of guilt or colonial agency, that I argue is alive and well in contemporary schools and formalized teacher training programs, yet we ignore its deep historical roots as well as its current existence. What was once described as maternalistic duty to rescue and civilize "ill-bred" children, first via the formation of women's organizations and foreign missionary societies, and soon after as teachers at home and abroad, has imbedded itself ideologically in the imagining of teachers throughout history, heard contemporarily in refrains such as "teaching is my calling" or "I teach because I love my kids." While teaching is no longer referred to as "doing the Lord's work," it is nonetheless revered, especially among white and middle-class teachers, as a selfless, heroic calling from a higher power. It is imperative to highlight the connections between historical and contemporary motivations behind this specific type of altruistic women's work, while also making visible the hidden work of white womanhood, then and now, in building and maintaining the white nation-state. To do this, I will propose a theory of "benevolent whiteness" that is deeply rooted in US colonialist educational history, and which persists to the present day.

Theorizing Benevolent Whiteness

Thus far, I have used existing theory to demonstrate how important it is to make visible the permanence of the trope of heroic maternal labor that relies on what I am calling "benevolent whiteness" in education. I have offered a brief historical explanation for the conflation of mothering and teaching as women's godly work, which I have proposed as a discursively constructed concept that persists to the present day, and which is an important and unrecognized foundation that undergirds race- and gender-based inequities in school discipline trends. I have also suggested connections between benevolent whiteness as an answer to a holy calling, and its specific and intentional role in furthering the US white nation-state.

My theorization of benevolent whiteness comes from the desire to re-center whiteness, and a specifically gendered whiteness, to make it visible and thus to destabilize white supremacy as the dominant ideology and system of power in the United States, to name it as a constant during the development of organized schooling throughout the 19th century; to be able to view benevolent whiteness ideologically, historically, and structurally in hopes that we can trace its persistence through schooling and interrogate its presence, rather than spend time paying attention to questions of individual teachers' commitments to anti-racism, equity, multiculturalism, and so forth. That is to say, the desire here is to take the focus off of individual teachers as potentially "racists" or "not racist" (which is where in my experience the conversations often lead), and to locate ourselves as educators as participants within a complex web that long predates us, and to therefore begin talking about that web, what it is doing, who it is harming, how we are sustaining it regardless of our intentions, and, most importantly, how we can begin to dismantle it for the benefit of our students and families.

In theorizing benevolent whiteness in education, I define whiteness following Leonardo (2009); I recognize and stress the importance of separating *white people*, a socially constructed identity generally assigned to those with white skin, from *whiteness*, a racial discourse and "structural valuation of skin color, which invests it with meaning regarding overall organization of society" (2009, p. 92). This differentiation is crucial to my theorization of benevolent whiteness because it allows for the fluid nature of race and gender, thus leaving room for the reification/reproduction/performance of benevolent whiteness by those who might not necessarily self-identify as white. While benevolent whiteness as a feminized arm of settler colonial violence has been carried out by white women historically, its legacy has impacted the field of education, and specifically the field of teacher education, in a way that makes indelible its mark on the profession. In other words, the way most of us have experienced schooling as students in the United States has been infused with the values of 19th-century white middle-class Protestant morality, and colonialist white supremacist suppression and oppression of Black and Indigenous populations. Thus, we must analyze the ways in which we teach pre-service teachers, the ways in which we envision the roles of teachers, and the ways in which visual and behavioral markers of the "proper" student subjects are deeply steeped in arcane traditions, to interrogate properly the racialized discipline gap and other inequities facing students of color in US schools.

My theorization of benevolent whiteness is based on analysis of the above-mentioned archival sources and the author's unpublished ethnographic data that have been distilled down to several key characteristics. Primarily, my definition of benevolent whiteness is that it is gendered feminine and operates through formalized schooling carried out by teachers from outside of the students' home community, where in most cases the students are of color and the teachers are white women. Historically, and at its start, missionary women carried out the work of benevolent whiteness. Contemporarily, this work is continued through programs such as Teach For America and its legacy, well documented in best-selling books and critically acclaimed movies such as *Dangerous Minds* (Smith, 1995) or *Freedom Writers* (LaGravenese, 2007). White (usually) female teachers enter into a chaotic urban school and are able to do the job that no one else (read: no Black or Brown teacher) was able to do.

This point leads to the second characteristic of benevolent whiteness: it literally and figuratively displaces teachers (and parents) of color within school communities, replacing them with heroic white teachers who "know better" how to reach/teach children of color. In the literal sense, this displacement has occurred in Black communities beginning with the Reconstruction South, during which northern white missionary women sought to "bring light to the darkness" by educating the "freedmen"; the most contemporary example of this literal displacement is post-Katrina[4] New Orleans, where all 7,000 plus of the city's teachers were fired, reducing the once predominantly Black teaching force (72% in 2004) to just 49%, and converting nearly all public schools into charters now flooded by transient Teach For America teachers (Barrett & Harris, 2015). Contemporarily, benevolent whiteness figuratively displaces teachers of color through the appropriation of techniques stolen from communities of color, for which communities of color are often penalized, including hip-hop pedagogy, physical movement strategies, handshakes, spoken word and musical performances, and so on.

Figuratively speaking, benevolent whiteness seeks to displace parents of color through ideological whitewashing of the ideal, proper woman and mother. For example, in Hawai'i white women were tasked with "educating" and converting the royal women; white women were used to access female ali'i (royalty) who distrusted male missionaries (Grimshaw, 1989). Their charge was to convince the ali'i to accept Christianity and its gender roles, and by proxy to accept a Protestant work ethic and a capitalist understanding of land ownership. The method for this transition, also used in countless prior colonial outposts, is to replace the Indigenous mother (figuratively) by transforming her into a pseudo-white, middle-class, Protestant mother (or as close to this as possible).

In Indigenous education, the displacement of parents has occurred both literally (in boarding schools) and figuratively. Retelling the story of a child re-named "our own Florence," Elaine Goodale Eastman analyzed the girl's father as simply not knowing better because he refused to send his daughter to the government day school. Rather than respecting a father's wishes (which would have required her viewing him as a real parent in the first place), Eastman fondly retold the story of how she lured Scarlett Ball to her school with "baskets of inviting food" and then enrolled the child in school on her own. Within two years of schooling, Scarlett was appropriately assimilated by Eastman's standards – in this case because she began pushing her father toward Christianity. Despite his refusal to convert, and based on no more than a lukewarm sentiment that his "seed had grown" from schooling, Eastman joyously announced that the "one time skeptic father is ever-grateful" for her intervention into his family, bypassing his parental authority, and converting a child she lured away through trickery.

The third identifying characteristic of benevolent whiteness is its roots in a multidirectional salvation: the need to simultaneously save peoples whose salvation would always remain incomplete, as well as saving the self. Historically, it should be remembered that the impetus for Protestant missions was first to demonstrate selfless service to God, thus leading to one's own salvation, with a secondary goal of bringing as many other "dark souls" toward the light, thus saving them as well. This salvation proved to be a difficult, if not impossible, project as, I argue, it was never imagined to be an attainable goal.

Contemporarily, this heroic fantasy is expressed as a desire to save/serve "underprivileged" (also marked as poor, urban, diverse, etc.) students, while lacking a political economic analysis of why those communities are underprivileged in the first place (i.e., a more nuanced understanding of white communities as "over-privileged" due to the theft of political and economic privileges from communities of color). Regardless of decade or geographic location, missionary women's writings all echoed a similar commitment to the idea that their salvation depended on their saving others. Many journals opened with early reflections on heeding the proverbial call and, after careful deliberation and weighing the horrific risks, ultimately always choosing the "Lord's will."

Elaine Eastman notes throughout her memoirs that she found her path to salvation through saving others (e.g., teaching). She reiteratively marks herself a savior, wondering rhetorically – for example, upon finding an abandoned government schoolhouse on Sioux land – "who would open the inhospitable doors of the waiting schoolhouse and ring the silent bells [if not her]?" This echoes the nearly identical sentiment made by missionary Lucy Thurston on her way to "save" the Kanaka Maoli of Hawai'i. Positioning herself on the side of assimilation in lieu of extinction regarding the "Indian problem," without wondering or caring why the schoolhouse sat abandoned and unwanted in the first place, Eastman balanced her proclaimed love for the Sioux people and culture with a firm stance that their culture was inferior and necessarily dying out. By hurrying that process along, Eastman was, by her rationale, saving Sioux lives and their nation, ironically, by attempting to erase them.

The final characteristic of benevolent whiteness is its operation through a language of "love," which I argue is an act of settler colonial violence when invoked by missionary teachers toward colonized and otherwise oppressed peoples. In Eastman's memoirs, for example, she speaks repeatedly of her love (a generally maternalistic and patronizing love) for the Dakota Sioux, often cited as a source or evidence of knowledge – that is "knowing" them and what is best for them (when conversing with Congress, for example). "We who loved them moved among them as freely and with as much confidence as ever," she claims, in response to the idea that the United States should fear another Indigenous uprising. She continues, now contradicting any claim of genuine love, that "only a handful of hopeless and desperate men" would consider rising up against the United States now that the "Sioux had been thoroughly 'conquered' in the 1870s" (Eastman, 1978, pp. 145–146). Again, she cites her love in a similarly contradictory statement: "We who really knew and loved the Sioux were convinced that, with patience and redress of their grievances, the sane and loyal majority might safely be counted upon to bring a fanatical few to their senses" (Eastman, 1978, p. 155).

Not surprisingly, much of the writing left behind by 19th-century missionary teachers regardless of geographic location echoes Eastman's refrains; their diaries and letters are replete with reference to love as the impetus behind what are, in reality, violent acts of settler colonialism (separation from family, erasure of Indigenous culture and language, indoctrination into middle class, Protestant, capitalist values, etc.). The language of love in contemporary educational discourse persists as a common trope. Teaching continues to be revered as a "calling" despite its contemporary decoupling from religion, and it is not uncommon to hear teaching credential candidates and veteran teachers alike explaining their career choice in loving terms (over practicality, material benefits, or being intellectually or academically well suited for it): they do it "out of love."

In understanding "love language as colonial violence" in its most reductive sense, I am referring to the ways in which teachers participate in settler colonialism through the discourse of "doing this for your own good," disciplining because they "love their students" and because they "want and know what is best" based on a narrow and antiquated idea of what success looks like in a capitalist society. One of the dangers in this comes from the power of love language to obfuscate complicity in colonial violence. This obfuscation is as present in contemporary faculty meetings as it is in the archives under analysis in this book. When love language is invoked in this manner, it isn't a genuine love, but rather a manipulative countermeasure meant to deflect from self-reflection or interrogating one's participation in oppressive behaviors or outcomes. It's the logical fallacy "If I am this (loving), I cannot also be that (oppressive)."

Contemporary educators must, then, have our eyes opened to the conscious or unconscious ways in which we daily reproduce an educational system in which heroes are needed in the first place. Benevolent whiteness depends on the "willful defiance"[5] of white women who insist that they are not racist, are not a part of racist policy implementation, that they are one of the "good ones," and therefore that they are incapable of coterminously being in any way at fault while they are doing the good work of saving "less fortunate" children from their communities and themselves. It, of course, also depends on the active or passive participation of educators of color who are brought up in the same school systems and under the same cultural norms and values that determine what we understand to be the proper student-subject, which we can impose very easily upon our students.

Beyond simply naming and understanding benevolent whiteness as the inescapable foundation of US schooling, throughout this book I encourage readers to find inspiration in the ways in which Black and Indigenous peoples survive and thrive despite the violence we face, whether under the guise of lovingly heroic intentions or through the more legible violence of the state and some of its citizens. It is through this framework of resiliency that we should imagine our futures as a people, as educators, as creators of new and renewed ways of schooling and learning, just as Black and Indigenous peoples have always done.

Notes

1 Here I follow Freire's (2003) conception of *conscientização*, roughly translated to "conscientization" or "acquiring a critical consciousness." Such an acquisition works toward liberation and requires both oppressors and the oppressed to be aware of and take action against dominant social myths and societal, political, and economical oppression.
2 "Commonsensical" in the Gramscian sense: un-interrogated and uncritically absorbed by the masses.
3 See, for example, Bushnell's *Christian Nurture* (1916), Beecher's *A Treatise on Domestic Economy, for the use of Young Ladies at Home and at School* (1841), Cobb's *The Evil Tendencies of Corporal Punishment: As a Means of Moral Discipline in Families and Schools, Examined and Discussed* (1847), and Sigourney's *Letters to Mothers* (1839).
4 Hurricane Katrina was the costliest, and one of the top five deadliest, hurricanes, in U.S. history. Katrina lasted from August 23, 2005, to August 31, 2005, and resulted in 1,837 fatalities, including that of the Louisiana public school system.
5 I use this term here intentionally, and somewhat ironically, calling attention to the catchall educational code category for which roughly half of all Black students are suspended.

References

Acker, S. (1995). Gender and teachers' work. *Review of Research in Education, 21*(1), 99–162.
Adams, D. W. (1995). *Education for extinction: American Indians and the boarding school experience, 1875–1928.* Lawrence: University Press of Kansas.
Althusser, L. (1971). *Lenin and philosophy.* B. Brewster (Trans.). New York, NY: Monthly Review Press.
Apple, M. W. (1985). Teaching and "women's work": A comparative historical and ideological analysis. *Teachers College Record, 86,* 445–473.
Barrett, N., & Harris, D. (2015). Significant changes in the New Orleans teacher workforce. *Education Research Alliance for New Orleans.* Retrieved January 20, 2016, from : http://educationresearchalliancenola.org/publications/significant-changes-in-the-neworleans-teacher-workforce
Beecher, C. E., & Katherine Golden Bitting Collection on Gastronomy (Library of Congress). (1841). *A treatise on domestic economy: For the use of young ladies at home, and at school.* Boston, MA: Marsh, Capen, Lyon, and Webb.

Blum, E. J. (2005). *Reforging the white republic: Race, religion, and American nationalism, 1865–1898.* Baton Rouge: Louisiana State University Press.

Brodhead, R. H. (1988). Sparing the rod: Discipline and fiction in antebellum America. *Representations, 21,* 67–96.

Bushnell, H. (1916). *Christian nurture.* New York, NY: Charles Scribner's Sons.

Cavanagh, E., & Veracini, L. (2013). Editors statement. *Settler Colonial Studies, 3*(1), 1. doi: 10.1080/18380743.2013.768169.

Clifford, G. J. (1989). Man/women/teacher: Gender, family, and career in American educational history. In D. Warren (Ed.), *American teachers: Histories of a profession at work.* New York, NY: Macmillan.

Cobb, L. (1847). *The evil tendencies of corporal punishment as a means of moral discipline in families and schools, examined and discussed: In two parts.* New York, NY: M.H. Newman & Co.

Coloma, R. S. (2012). White gazes, brown breasts: Imperial feminism and disciplining desires and bodies in colonial encounters. *Paedagogica Historica, 48*(2), 243–261.

Eastman, E. G. (1978). *Sister to the sioux: The memoirs of Elaine Goodale Eastman, 1885–1891.* Lincoln: University of Nebraska Press.

Foucault, M. (1977). *Discipline and punish: The birth of the prison.* New York, NY: Vintage Books.

Freire, P. (2003). *Pedagogy of the oppressed.* (Rev. ed.). New York, NY: Continuum.

Grimshaw, P. (1989). *Paths of duty: American missionary wives in 19th-century Hawaii.* Honolulu: University of Hawaii Press.

Grumet, M. (1988). *Bitter milk: Women and teaching.* Amherst: University of Massachusetts Press.

Jacobs, M. D. (2005). Maternal colonialism: White women and indigenous child removal in the American West and Australia, 1880–1940. *Western Historical Quarterly, 36*(4), 453–476. doi:10.2307/25443236.

LaGravenese, R. (Director). (2007). *Freedom writers.* Hollywood, LA: [Film]. MTV Films.

Leonardo, Z. (2002). The souls of white folk: Critical pedagogy, whiteness studies, and globalization discourse. *Race Ethnicity and Education, 5*(1), 29–50.

Leonardo, Z. (2009). *Race, whiteness, and education.* New York, NY: Routledge.

Leonardo, Z., & Boas, E. (2013). Other kids' teachers: What children of color learn from white women and what this says about race, whiteness, and gender. In Lynn, M., & Dixson, A. D. (Eds.), *Handbook of critical race theory in education* (pp. 313–324). New York, NY: Routledge.

Montgomery, S. E. (2009). Why men left: Reconsidering the feminization of teaching in the nineteenth century. *American Educational History Journal, 36*(1), 219–236.

Rousseau, J. J. (1768). *Emilius; or a Treatise of education.* Translated from the French, etc (Vol. 1). A. Donaldson.

Rury, J. (1989). Who became teachers? The social characteristics of teachers in American history. In D. Warren (Ed.), *American teachers* (pp. 9–48). New York, NY: Macmillan.

Sedlak, M. W., & Schlossman, S. (1986). *Who will teach? Historical perspectives on the changing appeal of teaching as a profession.* Santa Monica, CA: Rand Corporation Top of Form

Sigourney, L. H. (1839). *Letters to mothers.* New York, NY: Harper & Brothers, Cliff Street.

Smith, J. (Director). (1995). *Dangerous minds.* USA: [Film]. Hollywood Pictures.

Stoler, A. L. (2003). Tense and tender ties: The politics of comparison in (Post) colonial studies. *Itinerario, 27*(3–4), 263–284.

Strober, M. H., & Lanford, A. G. (1986). The feminization of public school teaching: Cross-sectional analysis, 1850–1880. *Signs, 11*(2), 212–235. Retrieved from http://www.jstor.org/stable/3174046

Welter, B. (1966). The cult of true womanhood: 1820–1860. *American Quarterly, 18*(2), 151–174.

Wolfe, P. (1999). *Settler colonialism and the transformation of anthropology: The politics and poetics of an ethnographic event.* London: Cassell.

2

WOMAN ON A MISSION

Lucy Goodale Thurston

Jan. 29, 1820. — I must not, I will not repine. Even now, though tears bedew my cheeks, I wish not for an alteration in my present situation or future prospects. When I look forward to that land of darkness, whither I am bound, and reflect on the degradation and misery of its inhabitants, … all my petty sufferings dwindle to a point, and I exclaim, what have I to say of trials, I, who can press to my bosom the word of God, and feel interested in those precious promises which it contains.

– Lucy Goodale Thurston, Missionary to Hawai'i

This chapter tells the story of the feminine arm of empire as flexed by women of the American Board of Commissioners for Foreign Missions (ABCFM), with a focus on the life and works of missionary Lucy Goodale Thurston (1795–1876). In considering the role of white womanhood in general, and that of Lucy Thurston specifically, this chapter asks how we can begin to see the discursive construction of a benevolent whiteness – a cult of true womanhood – that characterizes itself as wholly benevolent, innocent, and salvation-oriented, whose remnants are still evident in contemporary narratives about schooling and "saving" students of color. Lucy's story gives us insight into the impetus behind white women teaching Indigenous children (and adults, who were perceived as children) in the 19th century, and in a more general way into the minds of women regardless of era who are "called" into teaching with hopes of saving Black and Brown children from themselves and their families. Further, the work of Lucy and her contemporaries as evidenced by their own diaries and subsequent histories and biographies makes clear the conflation of evangelicalism with teaching: schools functioned as a tool with which to spread Christianity to "heathen" populations while simultaneously furthering US white middle-class values of capitalism and imperial domination in the name of enlightenment.

DOI: 10.4324/9781003201809-3

These qualities born alongside organized schooling are deeply embedded in the role of the female teacher, amalgamated to a point where they cannot be individuated or decoupled from the white female teacher's identity without explicit work and intention.

Lucy Goodale, aged 23, wrote the quote that opens this chapter while aboard the brig *Thaddeus* during the first American Board of Commissioners for Foreign Missions' (ABCFM) trip to the Kingdom of Hawai'i. After weighing the potential hardships and considerable dangers she would likely face living among heathens, she decided she would "risk everything" in order to "be given to the noble enterprise of carrying light to the poor benighted countrymen of Obookiah"[1] (Thurston, 1934). This theme of great personal suffering and martyrdom necessary for the sake of heathen salvation and enlightenment runs throughout missionary women's diaries and letters, and is a common refrain among their contemporary peers and lay countrypersons alike. Missionary Fidelia Coan described adult Kanaka as "poor children who are as sheep without a shepherd," declaring herself just the shepherd they needed to overcome their godless ways.[2] Contemplating a marriage proposal (and immediate mission to Hawai'i) from the formerly unknown Garrett Judd, Laura Fish proclaimed, "I feel that I am placed in the most trying circumstances. If it is the Lord's will, I am ready to go." Nine days later she declared, "'The die is cast.' I have in the strength of the Lord, consented Rebecca-like – 'I WILL GO,' yes, I will leave friends, native land, everything for Jesus" (Judd Family, 1903, pp. 26–28). Likening themselves to the biblical Rebecca, chaste and pious, God's chosen instruments, women from across New England sought teaching positions at home and around the globe in the name of "doing the Lord's work."

It is important to illuminate and interrogate this discourse of women's selfless and self-proclaimed heroism for several reasons. Primarily, it demonstrates the precise moment in time during which white womanhood became conflated with innocent heroism (although historically it has always been symbolic of innocence). Secondly, paying attention to white missionary women's voices makes visible the intersection of the putting into discourse the imagined benevolent teacher/savior role of white women with the larger, presumably masculine project of the US Global Empire and white supremacy;[3] thirdly, because it demonstrates a certain type of white woman drawn to teaching, and the discourse around teaching as a calling, from the beginning of formalized schooling and continuing to the present. Further, it is highly important and relevant that we read missionary women's words through a lens of gendered whiteness, as they (the women and their writing) were far more influential in the colonization of Hawai'i and the furthering of a discursive "benevolent whiteness" than published history has previously acknowledged.

Missionary women (and men) were required to keep extensive written records in the form of letters (to family, funders, and church) and private journals. Many of them additionally hand-copied their letters home into a bound journal prior to mailing. These writings were widely read by contemporaries during the 19th century, and many were later published into what now serves as the main written record of this period in US and Hawaiian history. As such, it is important to reread these works with a focus on white supremacy, and particularly a gendered analysis of white supremacy. Through such a lens, we can adjust the dominant discourse on the history of United States-Hawai'i relations, as well as our collective conception of the roles of white women in the US imperial project, and in schooling children of color throughout history to the present.

To understand further the agency held by missionary women without reducing them to oppressed and innocent participants in capitalist patriarchy, we must shed light on the impetus behind these women's missionary zeal, as well as the historical and social context of New England, the United States, and the Kingdom of Hawai'i. Lucy's inspiration, like most missionary women of her time, was not born of the ABCFM's new missionary programs; rather, many of these women were already trained as teachers and were in the process of heading west to help conquer the "new frontier" through the only avenue open to single women: the newly gendered feminine[4] profession of teaching. Juliette Montague and Louisa Clark had plans to travel west to teach, while Sybil Bingham and Lucia Ruggles were already employed as teachers in New England. All four women's letters and diaries, along with those of missionaries Mercy Partridge Whitney, Clarissa Lyman, Laura Fish Judd, and Lucy Goodale Thurston, spoke of their duty toward "selfless sacrifice" through teaching and spreading the gospel long before they were made aware of the ABCFM proposed Hawai'i mission (Grimshaw, 1989; Zwiep, 1991). For Lucy and others, the news of a missionary excursion to Hawai'i simply came at the right time, and seemed to offer a guaranteed way into gaining independence, agency, and heroism unlike what had hitherto been available hitherto for women in the United States. Feminized heroism in God's name was a path they were already walking, from which they would otherwise likely have ended up with them teaching "savages" in any number of continental locations: the expanding occupied Indian territory, and/or children of frontiersmen, or children in their home territory of New England. The seeds of salvation were already deeply planted within the hearts and minds of these young, educated white women; the ABCFM simply provided the women a soil in which their dreams and godly obligations could grow.

Background: Social and Political Context – New England

This first of many uninvited missions from New England to the Kingdom of Hawai'i was inspired in great part by the antebellum reform movements sweeping the nation: abolitionism, temperance, women's rights, and evangelicalism. Reform movements of the early 19th century found their genesis in three main phenomena: (1) economic change: the growing economy and its resulting production of the middle class to which most reformers belonged, (2) spiritual change: the "Second Great Awakening," (3) and cultural change: the women's rights movement, which grew out of abolitionism.

The rapidly growing economy of antebellum America produced a new middle-class while raising the standard of living for the already wealthy upper classes concentrated in primarily urban areas. For the rest of the country, the increase in industrial economies created low-paying, low-security, and often-dangerous employment for immigrants and the poor, including women and children. Those few who became wealthy through industrialization believed in and promoted the bootstrap mentality of hard work and self-discipline as key to success in the new economy. From their perspectives, the poor could easily share in the economic reward with a little more hard work and a lot less drinking. Combining this mindset with their Christian faith, many middle- and upper-class men and women (though predominantly women) were quick to join the temperance and other reform movements of the early 19th century.

The "Second Great Awakening" was a swell of Protestant evangelical revivalism flooding the United States in the first quarter of the 19th century. This new religious revival brought thousands of converts into the church, all fueled with the belief that their main duties to God and man included the eradication of sin, and a dedication to Biblical perfectionism for themselves and anyone they might convert. Conversion and specifically spreading the light among dark nations was a core tenet of 19th-century evangelical Protestantism, with one's sole purpose in life being the forced conversion and salvation of all the world's peoples. In the 19th century, conversions were largely contained within New England via regional traveling preachers and large religious gatherings or "camps" during which the devout could affirm their fervor while also bringing in potential converts. Of the thousands of new converts, far more were women than men. This led to a "feminization of religion" (Zwiep, 1991, pp. 10–11) previously unseen, which occurred coincidentally alongside the feminization of the teaching profession.

This is an important point to which I will return throughout this chapter, and throughout the book: two main facets of middle-class white womanhood were forged at the same time, during the period of the United States' greatest imperial expansion across the continent and the globe. These facets were then applied to define an ideal student/citizen subject, and used as a standard by which to judge morality writ large regardless of location, socioeconomic status, or desire to be included in this new and impossible ideal. Further, the concomitant feminization of religion and teaching led to a conflation of evangelical values and the ideals of missionary salvation with the 19th-century middle-class belief in teaching as women's work (Welter, 1966; Zwiep, 1991). It is this moment of putting into discourse the mother/savior/teacher trope and its immortal melding into the teaching profession that I intend to make visible, and to question as a valid mentality with which to teach diverse populations in the 21st century (or at any time, for that matter).

A third and coinciding movement working alongside the religious fervor of the Second Great Awakening was the nascent women's rights movement.[5] The movement was inspired somewhat unintentionally by the trope of "True Womanhood," a moniker given retroactively by contemporary historians, taken from the title of Barbara Welter's 1966 essay, "The Cult of True Womanhood." Welter describes the four pillars of True Womanhood as piety, purity, submissiveness, and domesticity, all of which were crucial to not only a woman's identity, but to the upholding of the nation and the (white) race. Through this trope, white women represented a moral standard that held constant, and held the family and nation together, despite all other changes or challenges, all while remaining confined to the home as her microcosmic world. Woman, with a capital W, was defined and defended by the primary political and social influences of the 19th century: women's magazines, pamphlets, illustrated gift annuals, and religious literature (Welter, 1966), and as in contemporary times, most women could not meet these impossible standards. This led to (1) the reiteration of a belief that white middle-class women were the only "true women," and were thus the rulers by which to measure the rest of the world, and (2) a population of white middle-class women who spent their lives struggling to adhere to a perfection that would remain beyond their reach (Welter, 1966, p. 8). The latter, along with the former, gave rise to a group of newly empowered, sanctioned by God, white women who would soon reject True Womanhood and its conflicting understanding of women's roles, leading to the creation of an organized movement for women's rights, and the eventual destruction of the True Womanhood ideal.

True Womanhood held that woman was by nature the weaker sex, yet they were also inherently morally pure and as close to perfect as any human might aspire. This characterization led to understanding women as the ideal candidates to influence morally their children, their husbands, the nation, and later their maternalistic charges in colonial outposts on the continent and abroad. Yet women's domain remained confined to the home, while men's domain was quite literally anywhere (and everywhere) in the world. Women were charged with doing the heavy moral lifting of the nation from within their domestic spheres, specifically by raising the next generation of white, Christian, male capitalist Americans. Aching to be free of their restrictions as "hostages in the home" (Welter, 1966, p. 8), middle-class white women would soon use parts of the True Womanhood ideal to their advantage, as evidence supporting their claims for greater political and societal influence within 19th-century reform movements, while simultaneously rebelling against the idea that women were the weaker sex. After all, if women were morally perfect by God's own design, they certainly owed it to themselves and the world to participate more freely and powerfully in all aspects of society. Building on the one exception to the rule of "hostage in the home," that church work did not sully a woman's perfect nature, white women were able to discursively create a world within which their work was always already the work of God, inspired and sanctioned by His word and His implied reasoning behind creating one morally perfect gender.[6]

Middle-class white women, many of whom participated in some way in abolitionism, began building what has become known as "The" Women's Rights Movement. I capitalize "the" and surround it with quotes to signal the movement's disingenuous name as well as its exclusion of most of the US female population, specifically poor women and women of color.[7] Ironically, a key leader of the movement, Angelina Grimké, is often quoted as saying, "The investigation of the rights of slaves has led me to a better understanding of my own," (Grimké, 1836) as if there were a reciprocal relationship between the needs of middle-class white women (those who were doing the speaking) and enslaved or freed Black women, poor women, or other "fallen" women (those who were without voice or recognition as "true women" at all). Along with Grimké, in 1848 a group of largely abolitionist, largely white middle-class women held a convention in Seneca Falls, which resulted in the "Declaration of Sentiments," modeled after the Declaration of Independence but with all men/patriarchy in the place of King George as oppressor. The Declaration served as a manifesto of the new Women's Rights movement and serves as perhaps the first example of white womanhood positioning itself as uniquely oppressed without acknowledging its role within oppression. It is also reflective of the myopic view middle-class white women had of what was best and right for all women, based solely on their limited experiences of the world and their desire to break free of what they had likened to the chains of chattel slavery.

Prior to the organized movement for women's rights, white women made smaller, strategic moves toward agency and breaking free of the "hostage in the homes" requirements of True Womanhood, but by all accounts they remained comfortably within its confines as servants of God and their husbands prior to and during missionary service. This was the archetype for 19th-century missionary wives: a desire to serve God and man at all costs, a reputation for absolute moral purity, a belief that women's inherent roles in life were to spread light and the gospel across the globe (Grimshaw, 1989; Zwiep, 1991), and just the right (controllable) amount of inclination to adventure and freedom from the confines of 19th-century womanhood.

Background/Social and Political Context – Hawai'i

Most mainstream histories[8] of 19th-century Hawai'i, informed by the writings of the first missionaries to the kingdom, tell the story of a feudal people[9] recently freed from an oppressive kapu (taboo) system and thus "literally a 'people without a religion' – a condition unique in history" (Thurston, 1934). This is problematic for many reasons, not least of all because it is based solely on the words of haole[10] missionaries and their descendants, thus reflecting a gross misunderstanding of pre-contact Hawai'i governance, beliefs, traditions, and history. Firstly, the idea that Kanaka women and maka'āinana[11] were oppressed is based on a western understanding of both gender roles and spirituality, compounded by the idea that Calvinist missionaries saw their own religion as one that held women in the highest esteem, and one which would in fact save "savage" women from their men and their cultures. Ironically, women in the United States were in many ways afforded far less freedom and agency than Kanaka women and women in general in pre-Christian Hawai'i.

Secondly, the oversimplification involved in describing Hawaiian governance and land use as "feudal" reflects a Euro-American understanding of their own medieval ancestors' feudalism more so than it actually describes what existed in Hawai'i pre-contact and through the mid-19th century. Hawai'i's governance was never akin to what has historically been defined as feudalism: a social system in which the land is owned by the Crown, and all who resided upon the land were bound to the land and the Crown either in exchange for protection or as military protectors of the Crown. Under Kamehameha's reign, and as far back as Kanaka oral history recites, maka'āinana "neither owed military service to ali'i nor were they bound to the land." Maka'āinana were free to live anywhere in the islands, without obligation, and could move from one moku[12] to another at any time without repercussion. Kanaka believed that the more people an ali'i[13] had living under their protection, the greater their power and status among peers. Thus, the obligation to provide for the people fell on ali'i rather than an obligation toward ali'i held by maka'āinana. To fail to provide for the people in one's moku reflected poorly upon ali'i, signifying a loss of mana[14] and status (Trask, 1993, pp. 4–6). This is diametrically opposed to the relationship between medieval feudal peasants and their lords, and was by no means a system from which kanaka needed or wanted "freedom" as defined by the Protestant Church and US white supremacy.

Haole interpretation of kanaka culture, society, and governance, as well as the events leading up to the end of the traditional kapu[15] system was and remains filtered through the lens of white US missionaries. The moment in history is generally reduced to a simple interaction between two allegedly power-hungry women and the newly crowned young (20-year-old) King Liholiho. It was indeed the late Kamehameha III's favorite wife Ka'ahumanu who, upon the monarch's death, decreed that the old customs and taboos be broken via her influence over Liholiho. Upon his deathbed, Kamehameha made Ka'ahumanu kuhina nui,[16] thus anointing her with the highest power of any woman in the kingdom, as equal (or as some would argue as superior) to Kamehameha's son, the new King Liholiho. As haole history tells it, along with Liholiho's mother (High Chiefess Kina'u, a daughter of Kamehameha I), Ka'ahumanu convinced Liholiho to aid her in abolishing the kapu system, particularly the kapu that applied to herself and other women, beginning with the kapu around men and women eating in each other's company. The abolition of the kapu system would presumably result in personal and political gain for both women, thus making this seemingly manipulative first act of the new monarchy one based on selfishness and greed. Many haole scholars (Grimshaw, 1989; Zwiep, 1991) thus read the abolition of kapu as an act primarily about the two women wanting to have power on par with men, despite the fact that both women already held more power than anyone, male or female, in the islands (see Kauanui, 2008, 2018; Linnekin, 1990). Both Grimshaw and Zwiep celebrate the end to the kapu system as a win for women's rights, again misreading the complexity of the Kanaka situation through a lens colored by white feminist thought and missionary writings of history.

Hawaiian writings from the 19th century, intentionally forgotten articles and diaries written alongside missionaries' journals, tell a much more nuanced story. Additionally, contemporary authors informed by more than just the one-sided history of Calvinist missionaries provide us with a different perspective to consider.[17] Merry (2000) and Trask (1993), for example, demonstrate that the food kapu, 'ai kapu, was once a source of mana, protecting the people. Rules prohibiting men and women from mixed eating, and preventing women from eating certain foods that were either phallic in nature and/or associated with masculine power, were based on a centuries-old belief in protecting the mana of the male ali'i, rather than as an overly simplified misogynistic rule meant to keep women subservient. Ka'ahumanu's decision to invite Liholiho to publicly dine with her was based on an extension of this belief in the ali'i's mana being directly tied to the health and safety of the people. Kamehameha III was seen as pono, following and enforcing all kapu, and full of more mana than perhaps any ali'i before him, all of which were royal qualities meant to ensure the livelihood of the maka'āinana and the nation. Yet toward the end of Kamehameha's rule, the Kanaka were no longer protected in the ways they had been prior to haole contact. Upward of 150,000 Kanaka had died of violence, common illnesses, and more complex and devastating diseases, none of which had the same deadly effects on haole living in the islands. The kapu system was simply no longer doing its job. Ka'ahumanu and her ali'i nui might have thus decided to break the 'ai kapu because they surmised that free eating was a source of the haole's resistance to death from simple disease, and because although haole had ignored the 'ai kapu for decades in Hawai'i, they had never been struck down by the gods (Merry, 2000, p. 61; Silva, 2004, p. 29). Thus the idea of mixed eating was considered as not only something for which Kanaka would not be punished as was previously believed, but more hopefully that the end to the 'ai kapu would be the key to protecting Kanaka from further decimation and thus ensuring the continued existence of the Kanaka Maoli for generations to come.[18]

Despite haole interpretation of the women's roles in ending the 'ai kapu as purely manipulative, Kanaka history tells another story. Liholiho complied with his mother's request that he sit and eat with her in the presence of men and women, although he did so cautiously and afraid of the repercussions promised by kahuna and common lore. Soon after the shared meal, according to missionary journals and contemporary haole authors, Ka'ahumanu convinced Liholiho to destroy all heiau and religious symbols in Hawai'i as an act of acknowledging that the kapu system and its power no longer existed. Again, the more complex history as told by Kanaka scholars (Silva, 2004; Trask, 1993), and which is based on Hawaiian language newspapers and the writing of 19th-century Kanaka historians, argues that the heiau were destroyed by the kahuna out of obligation, as their spiritual duty, because the heiau were symbols of a kapu system that was no longer pono,[19] and which perhaps was thus contributing to mass death unlike any they had ever known. Whereas haole scholars describe a simple, yet calculated, decision made by two power-hungry women, carried out by a scared young king, resulting in chaos and the destruction of all things traditionally Hawaiian, a more balanced reading of Kanaka history suggests the kuhina nui acted with the intention of preserving the health and lives of the Kanaka people and sustaining the kingdom through what seemed like the most logical means at the time.

Regardless of the destruction of the kapu and religious powers of the past, Hawai'i was not the empty vessel waiting to be filled with Christian light that the missionaries made it out to be. Basic beliefs, traditions, and practices remained in place, as did the traditional division of land and labor. What missionary writers and contemporary haole historians fail to acknowledge is the dire health of the overall population, now decimated by haole diseases, which was much more influential in the ali'i and maka'āinana eventually accepting and promoting Christianity as a promise of eternal life for their people, not necessarily for themselves as individuals (Trask, 1993). Combining the anecdotal evidence that haole broke the 'ai kapu and were immune to disease and death with the missionaries promise of eternal life in Christianity, Ka'ahumanu and other ali'i eventually became open to the idea that conversion to Christianity might be the best way to save the Kanaka Maoli (Kame'eleihiwa, 1992; Merry, 2000; Trask, 1993).

It is also important to note that despite the historical misremembering of schools in Hawai'i as wholly foreign impositions "of essentially American designs," Noelani Goodyear-Ka'ōpua (2018) reminds us that this is simply not the case. What grew into the kingdom-wide (now statewide) public and private school system in Hawai'i was initially an equal partnership between Kanaka and haole. Outside of a formalized school system, she notes that "schools were not the first educational institutions in the islands. Native educational institutions based on apprenticeship, mastery, and community predated and survived the advent of Western-styled schooling in Hawai'i" (p. 40, endnotes). This history is rarely included in any contemporary writings on schooling in Hawai'i, yet its truth must be reiterated here so that we may have a nuanced understanding of the impetus behind and intentions of haole-led schooling in Hawaiʻi and so we might return to our own Indigenous ways of educating the lāhui as we work toward imagining new futurities.

Woman on a Mission: Lucy Goodale Thurston

The swell of 19th-century Christian conversion in New England meant there was no shortage of saviors in search of someone(s) to save. Committed to accessing their own salvation, devout Congregationalists were determined to fulfill their desires and obligations to spread their gospel across the globe. In 1819, they found their inspiration in the diary of a young Kanaka Christian convert named ʻŌpūkahaʻia (in English, referred to as Henry or Heneri Obookiah).

ʻŌpūkahaʻia was born in 1792 in the Kaʻū moku of Hawaiʻi Island, just three years before Kamehameha the Great won the Battle of Nuʻuanu Pali and conquered all the major islands of Hawaiʻi.[20] ʻŌpūkahaʻia's father served in the army of his moku's aliʻi nui who, like other local chiefs, hoped to reclaim their lands from Kamehameha who was still fighting on Oʻahu. In retribution, Kamehameha's soldiers returned to Hawaiʻi Island and slaughtered all who fought against him, along with their wives, children, and any family members who could be found. ʻŌpūkahaʻia was around ten years old when his parents were killed in front of him, and though he attempted to escape with his infant brother on his back, the baby was quickly killed and ʻŌpūkahaʻia was captured and given to the family of the soldier who killed his parents. Soon after, he was ransomed as apprentice to his kahuna nui[21] uncle. ʻŌpūkahaʻia, however, had other ideas, and planned to leave the islands as soon as he was able. This chance came when he signed onto a Yankee ship leaving Hilo for Alaska, China, and eventually landing in New York in 1809. ʻŌpūkahaʻia would never again see his homeland.

Shortly after he succumbed to "typhus fever" at the age of 26, ʻŌpūkahaʻia's memoirs were edited and published by Edwin W. Dwight, a graduate of Yale, and coincidentally also the person named in the memoirs as "discovering" ʻŌpūkahaʻia "weeping on the steps" of Yale, embarrassed and lamenting his lack of education. According to the memoirs, his homeland, the "Sandwich Islands," were desperate for spiritual guidance and the parental oversight only Christian missionaries could provide. Along with ʻŌpūkahaʻia's words, common knowledge, pithy as it was, painted Hawaiʻi as an exotic land populated by ignorant heathens and drunken, lascivious sailors. As the story has been retold (by haole missionaries and their descendants), ʻŌpūkahaʻia fought typhus just long enough to implore his Christian brethren to travel to Hawaiʻi to spread Christianity and literacy in hopes of saving his people from eternal damnation. His diary, *Memoirs of Henry Obookiah* (1819),[22] was widely read, with over 50,000 published copies in circulation. One might argue that it was second only to the Bible in importance and influence among New England's middle-class evangelicals. Within a year of its publication the ABCFM formed the "Sandwich Islands Mission," and applications poured in from across the east coast.

Seven men were chosen for the first mission to Hawai'i; however, their sense of moral duty and adventure was not enough to prepare them for the journey. It was the deeply held belief, based on prior missions to Tahiti, that single men in heathen land would be unable to resist the advances of the naked and sexually promiscuous natives of Hawai'i. As fortune would have it, one of the many saintly roles meant for white women in the 19th century included the salvation of white men and Brown women from each other and from themselves (Coloma, 2009, 2012; Jacobs, 2009). Thus, it was required that all missionaries be protected from temptation by way of marriage prior to their departure. Like many unmarried missionary-minded young men, in mid-September a 32-year-old scythe maker and Yale and Andover graduate, Asa Thurston, spread the word to family and church that he was seeking a pious, selflessly benevolent bride to join him in the "Sandwich Islands." Word soon reached a cousin of an already adventure-minded, and highly educated[23] Lucy Goodale, whose father quickly arranged a meeting between the young pair. Within a few days Asa had proposed to Lucy, and less than two weeks later they were married. By October 23rd, a mere 11 days post-marriage, the Thurstons began their 157-day journey to salvation.

In the fall of 1819, the first group of Calvinist missionaries set sail from Boston for Hawai'i aboard the tiny vessel *Thaddeus*. The group consisted of the Thurstons and six other married couples: the Binghams, the Holmans (a doctor and his wife), the Whitneys and the Ruggleses (teachers and their wives), the Loomises (a printer and wife), and the Chamberlains (a farmer, his wife and their five children). In addition to the Protestant missionaries, the company included four Kānaka Maoli who had been educated and converted to Christianity in Massachusetts, and who were returning home to spread the gospel among their people.

Throughout their difficult journey, the missionary women kept detailed diaries of their travels, as well as expressions of their hopes and fears for their new life ahead. The general theme of most journals was one of intense physical and spiritual hardship – the immeasurable personal cost of leaving the only home they had ever known (referred to often as "their native land")[24] to travel to distant heathen lands, the arduous journey and near-constant seasickness, and the future threat of living under the kapu[25] system and its death penalty for seemingly endless offenses. Offsetting the chorus of hardship and uncertainty was a repeated refrain on the value of and gratitude for a chance at selfless sacrifice.

Upon the *Thaddeus's* arrival off the coast of Hawai'i Island, Kanaka men and women swam and paddled out to greet the crew and their missionary passengers. Appalled by the near-nudity of "the Natives," Lucy Thurston returned to her cabin in tears to confide in her husband and journal: "After sailing 18,000 miles, I met, for the first time, those children of nature alone" (Thurston, 1934, p. 30).

She, along with her female shipmates, expressed deep disgust and revulsion toward the Indigenous population within minutes of their first visual encounter – prior to ever setting foot on Hawaiian soil. Following similar narrative treatment of Africans in the United States, this first crew of missionaries began the rhetorical production of Kanaka as simultaneously subhuman and childlike, a trope they would continue to further throughout their decades in the islands, despite living side-by-side with Kanaka and raising their children alongside them.[26] Wood (1999) discusses a discourse of the Kanaka as "dirty, depraved beasts" and "filthy, naked, wicked heathen," a "rhetoric of revulsion" (pp. 38–39), often tempered by a simultaneous rhetoric that infantilized the Indigenous population. In much the same way that European and US whites used this technique to argue for paternal power over African slaves, Christian missionaries represented the Indigenous population in this precise manner, in turn positioning themselves as necessary heroes (both to their funders and to contemporaries at home, and eventually in recorded history). Thurston further confided in her journal:

As I was looking out of a cabin window, to see a canoe of chattering natives with animated countenances, they approached and gave me a *banana*. In return I gave them a biscuit. "*Wahine maikai*," (good woman) was the reply. I then threw out several pieces, and from my scanty vocabulary said "*Wahine*," (woman.) They with great avidity snatched them up and again repeated, "*Wahine maikai*."

(Thurston, 1934, p. 30; italics in original)

Thus began her decades-long discursive construction of Kanaka as simple, animal-like (snatching treats tossed their way like dogs), and blindly faithful toward and adoring of herself and the other missionaries. Lucy's diaries are rife with examples of Kanaka falling over themselves with adoration and love for the missionary mother-hero, especially upon each of Lucy's returns to Hawai'i Island from trips to neighboring islands or the United States (Thurston, 1934).

Kanaka, who ventured out to meet and marvel at the white women[27] on the *Thaddeus*, brought gifts of food along with news that long-reigning King Kamehameha was recently deceased, and with his passing, the centuries-old kapu system had been dismantled. The missionaries immediately took this as a sign of their God's divine intervention, creating opportunity and need for the word of the gospel and a new Christian savior (to be found in both themselves and their God). Lucy Thurston rejoiced to find "a people without a religion" (Thurston, 1934, p. C), while her shipmates confessed to their journals and in letters home an equal joy: "the idol gods are burned!"; "Surely this is the Lord's doings and it is marvelous in our eyes"; "It seems as if the Lord had verily gone before us and that the Isles are even *now* waiting for his law"; "the Lord hath comforted his people, and ministered unto us an open and abundant entrance among the heathen" (Grimshaw, 1989; American Board of Commissioners for Foreign Missions, 1821, p. 111; Thurston, 1934; Zwiep, 1991). They had arrived just in time.

Throughout her life, the remainder of which was spent in Hawai'i, Lucy continued to keep detailed diaries and handwritten copies of letters she sent to family and funders in New England. Her story weaves in themes commonly found in the confessional writing of her contemporaries: unbearable hardship made worthwhile by the promise of eternal salvation, a motherly love for the childlike Natives ("Think of children, cut off from the benefits of sanctuary, of schools, of associates: of children thus exiled, I am the mother ... they say 'you are our father, our mother: tell us what to do.'") who returned that love tenfold, and the ongoing difficulty of raising white children in a heathen land no matter how Christian it had supposedly become.

Soon after their arrival in Hawai'i, the Thurstons were given probationary permission to set up on the arid Kona side of Hawai'i Island in a small, one-room hut. They lived there for a brief seven months, after which they were allowed to move their mission home and church to Honolulu, where they lived for the next three years. During this time, Lucy gave birth to two children: Persis and Lucy (who later died as a child in New England). In Honolulu the Thurstons were able to more readily attempt their mission to convert the Kanaka population through first converting the ali'i. They met regularly with ali'i Liholiho (now Kamehameha II) and Kamāmalu, due more to of the ali'i's fascination with the haole missionaries than due to any power or influence they may have thought they held. The Thurstons worked tirelessly to convert the king and his wives, though they showed little interest in following either Protestant doctrine or New England customs. According to Lucy's diaries and letters home, their failure at converting the ali'i was not due to the Thurston's lack of effort or the Kanaka's disinterest in eternal salvation; instead, she cites alcoholism and innate laziness as the reasons for the failed conversion. This diagnosis quickly became "truth" in Hawai'i and New England, falling in line with white supremacist ideas regarding all other Indigenous and non-European populations with whom they had come into contact (Filipino, African, Native Americans, and so on).

Liholiho and Kamāmalu died soon after their failed conversion, contracting measles during a trip to London (July, 1825). The resulting change in Kanaka governance was mourned by the Thurstons, who saw themselves as trusted friends to the deceased ali'i, yet it was also celebrated as a new opportunity to once again attempt conversion of the maka'āinana by first converting their ali'i. By this time (1824) the Thurstons had returned to their home in Kona. Lucy's diaries tell a story of tireless work running the home and raising children leaving her husband free to do the work of preaching and converting Kanaka. Still fueled by their own desires to grow God's flock, Lucy and the other mission wives spent their days meeting familial obligations, and their evenings doing the work they imagined they had traveled across the world to do: proselytizing to and converting Indigenous women. Lucy wrote, "I am the house-keeper, the mother, and the domestic teacher. What time I can redeem from family cares, I give to our native females," (Thurston, 1934, p. 103). In addition to teaching her "grateful" and "eager pupils" the glory of eternal salvation, Lucy made it her main priority to teach Kanaka women how to be proper women and mothers according to New England Protestant values: "we tried to give them a standard of what was right," she wrote, "and began by endeavoring to form a healthy moral atmosphere in two rooms, eighteen feet square, where natives were allowed to tread" (Thurston, 1934, p. 90). She established regular women's meetings within which to do this work, hoping to bring light to the heathens by acting upon the women and mothers who would, it was hoped, share their new Protestant beliefs and influence with their as yet unsaved children and husbands. She prided herself on having taught thousands of Kanaka wāhine "scriptures and civilized comportment" in the course of just a few years.

During these early years in Hawai'i, Lucy's diaries tell of her unbearable loneliness, feeling overworked as a domestic servant (yet constructing her work as God's will), and deep conflict over her children's future welfare living in a heathen land. "We are willing to come and live among you, that you may be taught the good way," she writes, "but it would break our hearts to see our children rise up and be like the children of Hawaii" (Thurston, 1934, p. 129). Contemporary white feminist authors retell Lucy's story with an equal sense of pity and feminist pride, applauding her tireless determination to be an equal part of the missionary work without analyzing the violence implicit in the mission (Grimshaw, 1989; Zwiep, 1991). They empathize with her decision in 1840 to send her children back across the ocean to be raised among proper (white) people, even while knowing this meant she would likely never see her children again. While they include some analysis of the racist hypocrisy of the missionaries' refusal to raise their children among the Natives, the underlying sentiment expressed by modern-day white female scholars remains the same as that of Lucy's contemporaries: it was a difficult (yet understandable) decision made by a loving, overworked, and wholly benevolent mother. Lucy's own words tell a similarly whitewashed story of Indigenous mothers applauding her decisions to segregate their children. She wrote:

> The heathen could see that it was such evidence of parental faithfulness and love, as was not known among them … I have often seen them shed tears, while contrasting our children with their own degenerate offspring"
> (Thurston, 1934, p. 128)

Despite Lucy Goodale Thurston's immediate and lifelong disgust toward and pity for "the dark minds of these untutored natives," she remained in the islands until her 1876 death at the age of 81. As one of the first and longest remaining missionaries in Hawai'i, Lucy has become somewhat legendary, as much as any woman in the missionary project could have been given what little attention has historically been paid to the "fairer sex." Attempts at writing missionary women back into history (Grimshaw, 1989; Thigpen, 2014; Zwiep, 1991) have lauded Thurston as an unsung hero,[28] celebrating the "feminist implications" of her desire to join the mission in the first place, as well as her lifelong commitment to suffering through great personal sacrifice in the name of heathen salvation. Yet by painting Thurston as a hero for feminism writ large, white feminist scholars once again mark feminism as a solely white terrain, and white womanhood as universal. What is more, they further the long-held trope of the white woman as *oppressed* by patriarchy, yet not *oppressive* to the Indigenous populations they lovingly and benevolently colonize and conquer. In so doing, contemporary scholars perpetuate missionary love language as colonial violence.

Conclusion

While most women missionaries shared a similar view of themselves as godly servants and innocent saviors, in this chapter I narrowed my focus on the words of Lucy Goodale Thurston for several reasons: (1) unlike most missionaries, she remained in Hawai'i all of her life, and kept detailed written accounts of her life, which were/are published and widely read, meaning her story has been the "truth" as understood by most historians and laypeople alike; (2) she is often lauded as a hero missionary, a hero to feminism, and written about contemporarily (Zwiep, Grimshaw) in an effort to "give her a voice" where she has been silenced by history. Ironically, by giving Thurston a voice (which she arguably already had, if not compared to male missionaries but compared to most white and Indigenous women of her time) the authors summarily silence the voices of the Kanaka Maoli, further amplifying the voices of whiteness and white womanhood in the story of schooling and what it means to be a teacher specifically among nonwhite peoples; and (3) being among the first missionaries, and the longest living in the islands, her journals provide the most complete picture of missionary women's lives in Hawai'i, but more importantly the most complete record of the discursive construction of benevolent whiteness. It was Thurston's dying wish (granted by her descendants and the ABCFM) that her words be spread across the continent, and her story of the Hawaiian Islands be known for generations to come. This chapter sought to reinterpret Lucy's story, to conduct a close reading of the putting into discourse a heroic white womanhood somehow separate from white supremacy and free of accountability, and to question her story's validity and its silencing of Indigenous voices both then and now.

In considering the role of white womanhood in general, and that of Lucy Thurston specifically, we can begin to see the discursive construction of a benevolent whiteness – a cult of true womanhood – that characterizes itself as wholly benevolent, innocent, and salvation-oriented. This leads us to ask what remnants of this are evident in contemporary narratives about schooling and saving students of color. Lucy's story gives us insight into the impetus behind white women teaching Black and Indigenous children (and adults, who were perceived as children) in the 19th century, and more generally a way into the minds of women regardless of era who are "called" into teaching with hopes of saving nonwhite children from themselves and their families. Further, the work of Lucy and her contemporaries as evidenced by their own diaries and subsequent histories and biographies makes clear the conflation of evangelicalism with teaching: schools function(ed) as a tool with which to spread Christianity to "heathen" populations while simultaneously furthering US white middle-class values of capitalism and imperial domination in the name of enlightenment. These qualities, born alongside organized schooling, are deeply embedded in the role of the female teacher, amalgamated to a point where they cannot be individuated or decoupled from the white female teacher's identity without explicit work and intention.

Toward that goal, I ask readers to complicate their understandings of "love" and "good intentions" and to consider how their desires to serve and save historically oppressed students reinforces and reproduces violent white supremacy. My hope is that a required first step is teachers understanding white supremacy as structural and ideological; it is the water we swim in and the air we breathe in the United States. Benevolent whiteness is only one of its incarnations, one head of the hydra that is white supremacy, yet it is one of the most dangerous because of its invisibility that normalizes it, and its untouchable status due to its being couched in language of love. Because of that, following bell hooks I ask teachers to exercise restraint with their use of "love" as a descriptor or a feeling when it comes to teaching their young students. As hooks instructs us, among so many other necessary lessons, "there can be no love without justice" (hooks, 2000) and therefore the word or the claims of "love" cannot simply be thrown around in this way, used as a shield to protect one from accountability for harmful impact despite intent. To be clear, this is not a call for teachers, particularly outsider teachers, to abandon love and caring for Black, Indigenous, and other children of color. It is instead a call for teachers to be mindful of and intentional with their use of love language in relations to those children, to better understand their impetus for choosing teaching as a career, and to reflect on their daily interactions in the classroom in relation to their claims to love their students. Furthermore, my hope is that we all understand that love itself is not enough. Ideally, once teachers begin to see themselves not simply as individual good or bad actors, but instead as participants in something structurally violent, we can then make inroads toward dismantling these structures and reimagining schooling, teaching, Black and Indigenous communities as holders of knowledge and ways of learning, and even our understandings of love.

Notes

1 Obookiah is the Anglicized name for Kanaka sailor and student 'Ōpūkaha'ia, famous in New England as an example of "how the heathen could be regenerated" (Zwiep, 1991, p. 14). Reverend Edwin Dwight's *Memoirs of Obookiah* (1818) sold over 50,000 copies throughout New England and was the inspiration for many applications to the ABCFM's Hawai'i missions.

2 Fidelia Coan to M. Robinson, 1/26/1838; cited in Grimshaw, 1989, p. 105.

3 Throughout this book, I use the term "white supremacy" not to describe hate groups or blatant Klan-like organizations we have come to associate with the term. Instead, I follow scholars of whiteness studies and critical race theory in understanding "white supremacy" as a systematic racial ordering that benefits those deemed white at the cost of oppressing people of color (Bonilla-Silva, 2010; Leonardo, 2004, 2009; Smith, 2006).

4 See Chapter 1 for a more extensive analysis of the feminization of teaching.

5 The Women's Rights Movement became an organized movement of the latter half of the 19th century, roughly forty years after the *Thaddeus* set sail for Hawai'i. Its genesis, however, was rooted as well as grown out of the same economic and cultural changes that inspired women's participation in foreign missions and in expanding their worlds both literally and politically.

6 I am working under the 19th-century belief that God is a "He" and that there are two distinct genders. I want to acknowledge my rejection of both ideas, while also realizing that though this book is meant to interrogate/challenge past notions of gender and patriarchy, there is insufficient room to address it in this regard.

7 For excellent analysis of the racism in the women's rights movement, see Ginzberg, L. D. (2009). *Elizabeth Cady Stanton: An American life*. New York: Hill and Wang.

8 See, for example, Daws' *Shoal of Time* (1968/1982), Kuykendall's *The Hawaiian Kingdom* (1938), and Fuchs' *Hawaii Pono* (1992/1961).

9 For a detailed analysis of western scholars' invention of feudalism in Hawai'i, see the first section in Part III of Haunani Kay-Trask's *From a Native daughter: Colonialism and sovereignty in Hawai'i*.

10 Haole literally translates to "foreigner." Early foreigners, usually white Europeans and US citizens, as well as Asian immigrants were initially referred to as haole. Contemporarily, white people are considered haole whether or not they are "foreigners" (newcomers) to the islands whereas Asians, whether recent immigrants or descendants of plantation workers, are referred to by their ethnic group (Japanese, Chinese, and so on).

11 Commoners: primarily laborers, fishermen, farmers, and so on.

12 District or land division.

13 Chiefs.

14 Spiritual or divine power.

15 The religious system of rules and prohibitions, particularly defining relationships between the ali'i and maka'āinana and haole. "Kapu" when used as an adjective or noun means "sacred" or "forbidden."

16 The Kuhina Nui was a unique position in Kanaka government, roughly translated as "co-regent," and had no equivalent in western governments of the day. "The Kuhina Nui held equal authority to the king in all matters of government, including the distribution of land, negotiating treaties and other agreements, and dispensing justice." http://ags.hawaii.gov/archives/centennial-exhibit/kuhina-nui-1819-1864/.

17 For a more thorough and Kanaka centered history of Hawai'i, see the introduction to Haunani-Kay Trask's *From a native daughter: Colonialism and sovereignty in Hawai'i*, (pp. 1–28), Dougherty (1992), Ī'ī and Barrere (1959), Kauanui (2008) Merry (2000), Silva (2004), and Trask (1993).

18 For an in-depth explanation of the kapu, see the translated writing of 19th-century Kanaka historian John Papa Ī'ī, *Fragments of Hawaiian History* (1959), David Malo's *Hawaiian Antiquities* (1903), and Samuel Manaiakalani Kamakau's *Ruling chiefs of Hawaii* (1961).

19 Righteous, moral, respectable, correct.

20 By 1810, Kaua'i and Ni'ihau were also united within the newly established Kingdom of Hawai'i.

21 High priest; also "Kahuna po'o."

22 This is not the same text as the book published later in 'Ōlelo Hawai'i (the Hawaiian language) in 1867 in New York: *Ka Moolelo o Heneri Opukahaia (The History of Henry Obookiah)*. The published book is based on the same English story, but is edited for errors, and includes further information gathered by Rev. S. W. Papaula in Kealakekua.

23 Lucy received significantly more schooling than most girls. With the support of her father, she attended and graduated from Bradford Academy, one of New England's first coeducational academies, and she later became a schoolteacher.

24 There is something to be said here regarding haole referring to North America as their own "native land," particularly as it relates to the speed with which they soon after referred to Hawai'i in the same regard, and referred to themselves as kama'āina (children of the land). *Cf.* Wood, *Displacing Natives: The Rhetorical Production of Hawai'i*.

25 Kanaka system of laws and prohibitions, including rules prohibiting women eating phallic shaped foods (bananas) or those associated with masculine energy, rules against men and women eating in each other's company, and rules prohibiting looking at or casting shadows upon certain ali'i or sacred spaces.

26 For a thorough analysis of white American women's attempts at separating Native from nonnative children, see Zwiep (1990) "Sending the Children Home: A Dilemma for Early Missionaries."

27 Although haole men from Europe and the United States had long been a presence in the islands, white women were a rare sight prior to 1820 as most explorers were male and the addition of women to missionary trips was a new ABCFM requirement meant to keep its white men from falling prey to insatiable Polynesian women.

28 Strange, yet unsurprising, as her grandson Lorrin A. Thurston (1857–1931) ended up as a leader of the 1893 overthrow of the Kingdom of Hawai'i, and her great-great-grandson, Thurston Twigg-Smith (recently dead as of July 2016), spent his twilight years fighting against the Hawaiian Sovereignty Movement. Lucy Goodale Thurston literally gave birth to the end of the Hawaiian Kingdom.

References

American Board of Commissioners for Foreign Missions. (1821). *The Missionary Herald.* Boston, MA: Published for the Board by Samuel T. Armstrong.

Bonilla-Silva, E. (2010). *Racism without racists: Color-blind racism and the persistence of racial inequality in the United States.* Lanham: Rowman & Littlefield Publishers.

Coloma, R. S. (2009). 'Destiny has thrown the Negro and the Filipino under the tutelage of America': Race and curriculum in the age of empire. *Curriculum Inquiry, 39*(2009), 495–519.

Coloma, R. S. (2012). White gazes, brown breasts: imperial feminism and disciplining desires and bodies in colonial encounters. *Paedagogica Historica, 48*(2), 243–261.

Daws, G. (1968/1982). *Shoal of time: A history of the Hawaiian Islands.* Honolulu: University Press of Hawaii.

Dougherty, M. (1992). *To steal a kingdom: Probing Hawaiian history.* Waimanalo: Island Press.

Fuchs, L. H. (1992/1961). *Hawaii pono: Hawaii the excellent: An ethnic and political history.* Honolulu: Bess Press.

Ginzberg, L. D. (2009). *Elizabeth Cady Stanton: An American life.* New York, NY: Hill and Wang.

Goodyear-Ka'ōpua, N. (2018). Indigenous oceanic futures: Challenging settler colonialisms and militarization. In Linda Tuhiwai Smith, Eve Tuck, & K. Wayne Yang (eds.), *Indigenous and decolonizing studies in education* (pp. 82–102). Abingdon: Routledge.

Grimké, A. E. (1836). *Appeal to the Christian women of the South.* New York, NY: American Anti-Slavery Society.

Grimshaw, P. (1989). *Paths of duty: American missionary wives in 19th-century Hawaii.* Honolulu: University of Hawaii Press.

hooks, bell. (2000). *All about love: New visions* (1st ed.). New York, NY: William Morrow.

Ī'ī, J. P., & Barrere, D. B. (1959). *Fragments of Hawaiian history.* Honolulu: Bishop Museum Press.

Jacobs, M. D. (2009). *White mother to a dark race: Settler colonialism, maternalism, and the removal of indigenous children in the American west and Australia, 1880–1940.* Lincoln: University of Nebraska Press.

Judd Family. (1903). *Fragments: Family record of the house of Judd.* Honolulu, privately published.

Kamakau, S. M. (1961). *Ruling chiefs of Hawaii.* Honolulu: Kamehameha Schools Press.

Kame'eleihiwa, L. (1992). *Native lands and Foreign desires: Pehea lā e pono ai?* Honolulu: Bishop Museum Press.

Kauanui, J. K. (2008). *Hawaiian blood: Colonialism and the politics of sovereignty and indigeneity.* Durham, NC: Duke University Press.

Kauanui, J. K. (2018). *Paradoxes of Hawaiian sovereignty.* Durham, NC: Duke University Press.

Kuykendall, R. S. (1938). *The Hawaiian Kingdom.* Honolulu: University of Hawaii.

Leonardo, Z. (2004). The color of supremacy: Beyond the discourse of 'white privilege'. *Educational Philosophy and Theory, 36*(2), 137–152.

Leonardo, Z. (2009). *Race, whiteness, and education.* New York, NY: Routledge.

Linnekin, J. (1990). *Sacred queens and women of consequence: Rank, gender, and colonialism in the Hawaiian Islands.* Ann Arbor: University of Michigan Press.

Malo, D. (1903). *Hawaiian antiquities: Mo'olelo Hawaii.* Honolulu: Hawaiian Gazette Co., Ltd.

Merry, S. E. (2000). *Colonizing Hawai'i: The cultural power of law.* Princeton: Princeton University Press.

Silva, N. K. (2004). *Aloha betrayed: Native Hawaiian resistance to American colonialism.* Durham, NC: Duke University Press.

Smith, A. (2006). Three pillars of white supremacy. In Incite! Women of Color Against Violence (ed.), *Color of violence: The Incite! anthology* (pp. 66–73). Cambridge, MA: South End Press.

Thigpen, J. (2014). *Gender and American culture: Island queens and mission wives: How gender and empire remade Hawai'i's Pacific world.* Chapel Hill: University of North Carolina Press.

Thurston, L. (Goodale) Mrs. 1795–1876 (1934). *Life and times of Mrs. Lucy G. Thurston: wife of Rev. Asa Thurston, pioneer missionary to the Sandwich islands, gathered from letters and journals extending over a period of more than fifty years. Selected and arranged by herself.* Ann Arbor: S. C. Andrews.

Trask, H. K. (1993). *From a Native daughter: Colonialism and sovereignty in Hawai'i*. Monroe, Maine: Common Courage Press.

Welter, B. (1966). The cult of true womanhood: 1820–1860. *American Quarterly, 18*(2), 151–174.

Wood, H. (1999). *Displacing natives: The rhetorical production of Hawaii*. Lanham: Roman & Littlefield Publishers.

Zwiep, M. (1990). Sending the children home: A dilemma for early missionaries. *Hawaiian Journal of History, 24*, 39–68.

Zwiep, M. (1991). *Pilgrim path: The first company of women missionaries to Hawai'i*. Madison: University of Wisconsin Press.

3

THE INVASION OF LIGHT AND LOVE

Laura Matilda Towne

> I have felt all along that nothing could excuse me for leaving home, and work
> undone there, but doing more and better work here. Nothing can make amends to
> my friends for all the anxiety I shall cause them, for the publicity of a not pleasant
> kind I shall bring upon them, but really doing here what no one else could do as
> well. So I have set myself a hard task.
>
> – Diary of Laura M. Towne, April 17, 1862, Beaufort, SC

Laura Towne (1825–1901) penned her earliest missionary diary entry by describing her new home, the "lovely nature" and the people, from white soldiers idling in the streets, to "odd" and "unintelligible negro children," to Black women who "begged us to stay, for 'seemed like they could n't be happy widout white ladies 'roun'." The perceived and (her own) potential future suffering coupled with the apparent lack of direction among the inhabitants of Beaufort and their newly arrived teachers sets the stage for Towne's clear sense of intense sacrifice and duty. She finds herself in an impossible quandary: by following her long-held desire to venture South as an abolitionist and missionary teacher, she leaves an immeasurable void back in Philadelphia, with work at home undone and friends suffering anxiety due to potential "publicity of a not pleasant kind." Yet, as she makes clear, despite her absence in Philadelphia causing great suffering for friends and family, there is no one other than Towne herself who can do the work needed in Port Royal, and that makes the sacrifice worthwhile. She has no choice; her duty is to God, the Union, and a recently abandoned but not yet freed Black population in need of salvation.

This chapter argues that an understanding of the genealogy of schooling in the United States, and a desire to imagine its decolonized futures, requires a nuanced understanding of the relationships between settler colonialism and anti-Blackness and the roles schools and teachers have played in supporting those structures.

DOI: 10.4324/9781003201809-4

It also makes visible in the ruptures and erasures how Black and Indigenous communities have historically and contemporarily created spaces of resistance and solidarity. Toward this end, BIPOC educational scholars, teachers, school leaders, and community members along with white accomplices are compelled and positioned to break free from the violent trappings of settler colonialism and anti-Blackness and bring forth multiple new educational futurities.

As in the previous and following chapters, it is imperative that we frame missionary women's confessional literature and its discursively constructed innocent heroism through a lens of benevolent whiteness to better understand the complexity of what otherwise is remembered as a wholly/holy innocent duty and calling. Whereas Chapter 1 delineates the precise moment during which white womanhood becomes conflated with innocent heroism in contrast to the more masculine duty of white men to venture forth with arms and conquer physically all frontiers, this chapter follows the spread of both tactics as equally necessary and violent arms of the same beast; two similar but distinctly necessary armadas in the army of whiteness (Leonardo & Boas, 2013). Through such an understanding, we are better able to understand white womanhood within what is otherwise categorized as a masculine project of US empirical expansion and maintenance of its own boundaries (i.e., getting the South back into the Union). Likewise, as with other missionary women under analysis in this text, Towne's words, what is written about her, and what is known about her missionary peers and predecessors further demonstrate the particular sort of 19th-century white woman drawn to teaching and missionary work as a godly duty and calling – a type not unlike those drawn to teaching today. Further, it is important that we read 19th-century women's confessional literature as more than simply the ramblings of white women oppressed under patriarchy, but rather as powerful agents discursively constructing benevolent whiteness and the inherently heroic roles necessary to restore the Nation, capitalism, empirical expansion, and, most importantly, God's will.

Towne's letters and diaries further demonstrate the discursive construction of an identity built upon of selfless sacrifice of missionary white women that was first deployed in the 1820s by missionaries to Hawai'i. More commonly known and read are the wealth of missionary men's writing tracing directly the connections between the AMA (American Missionary Association) ideological colonization of island nations under the US empire, Black education on the continent, and later Indian education for Americanization, particularly with the Armstrong family and its second-generation missionary son, Samuel Chapman Armstrong, founder of the AMA Hampton Normal and Agricultural Institute established in 1868 in Hampton, Virginia. Armstrong, a Union Army colonel and commander of US Colored Troops (USCT) during the Civil War, was the son of AMA missionaries in Hawai'i. Armstrong's experience commanding the 8th USCT is cited as his first moment of interest in Black welfare.[1] His experience growing up as a member of a missionary family, bearing lifelong witness to the AMA methods of schooling and Christianizing Kanaka Maoli, informed his beliefs in the purposes and possibilities of schooling for Black and (later) Indigenous peoples, stating: "It meant something to the Hampton School, and perhaps to the ex-slaves of America, that, from 1820 to 1860, the distinctly missionary period, there was worked out in the Hawaiian Islands, the problem of the emancipation, enfranchisement and Christian civilization of a dark-skinned Polynesian people in many respects like the Negro race" (Hampton Institute, 1893, p. 1). Following his missionary parents' methods, Armstrong designed Hampton to educate Black children by schooling "the head, the hand, and the heart," training students who would return to their communities to spread AMA ideologies and Christian capitalist beliefs and behavior among their people.

In the same way that missionary pedagogical methods and beliefs traveled across generations and geographies, Towne's writings present us with a parallel course through which heroic white female identity is written indelibly upon the teaching profession. It is important that we read her words, and those of other 19th-century missionary women "between the lines to complete the picture," as suggested by Rupert Holland, editor of the published *Letters and Diaries of Laura Towne*:

> The value of this diary and these letters lies in the personal note. They should be read as the story of a pioneer. It was no light task to leave home and friends to volunteer for service during wartime; it was even less light to stay in such service when the excitement was over and only the work remained. None but a spirit heroic in steadfastness could achieve such success. Yet heroism was not in Miss Towne's thoughts, simply the conviction that this was the work allotted her to do. We must read between the lines to complete the picture. The structure of daily incidents and thoughts is there, we can build the full life only if we read events with sympathy and understanding.

Through such a reading, we construct a revised identity, a more correct and nuanced role performed by white womanhood in the 19th century and beyond. We see instead the power of benevolent whiteness and its role in shoring up the white capitalist United States, particularly at a moment in time when the country was split in two and war was raging not for the sake of Black humanity, but to solidify Lincoln's Union. Further, we can better understand the methods through which benevolent whiteness works to discipline nonwhite peoples who are understood as something other than citizens, Americans, or human. Reading between the lines, taking into consideration the social and political context at the time, we are able to find something other than simply the innocent sacrifice and heroism Holland praises in Towne if we indeed read with "sympathy and understanding" for someone other than the already extolled missionary and her compatriots.

Social and Political Context: US Civil War (1861–1865) and Reconstruction (1865–1877)

Antebellum Black Education

Regardless of legal, economic, or political restrictions, free and enslaved Black people did everything in their power to become educated, either formally or in secret. Prior to 1831, there were few laws preventing Black education as there was no real understood need. Free Black people had long organized their own schools and reading groups for adults and children, many of which focused on literacy required to read the Bible as part of fully accessing their Christian religion. Likewise, many southern slave owners allowed or provided for education to their slaves who in turn taught others. All of this changed after Nat Turner's Rebellion in 1831, during which an estimated 60 white people were killed (whose deaths were avenged with the murders of over 200 Black people). Terrified white citizens blamed the rebellion on Turner being "too educated," turning him into the living embodiment of their fears of an educated Black public. After the rebellion, southern states made Black education and congregation without a licensed white presence illegal, and it remained so until the South lost the Civil War in 1865 (Anderson, 1988, p. 148). It was clear to both white and Black southerners, as well as their northern neighbors, that Black education was the antithesis to white supremacist oppression, and this clarity would directly influence the organization of Black educational futures post-emancipation.

Because the United States' common school movement began during slavery – roughly 25 years before the start of the Civil War – there was initially no need to think about, much less implement, an organized and federally funded education system for Black children in the US South. Unlike northern common schools' assimilationist goals of Americanization (creating a common white national identity) for near- and newly white immigrants, as well as missionary and government use of schooling as a tool for colonizing island nations, the idea of schooling Black people was a direct threat to white citizenship in most of New England, where educated Black people were already seen as economic competition.[2] If the primary goal of common schooling was creating a unified citizenry during a time when Black citizenship – not to mention humanity – was denied, even the most liberal reformers were well within their perceived moral rights to deny Black children access to publicly funded schools. Likewise, during the 19th-century white schooling boom, areas with independent Black schools, or worse yet integrated schools, were met with mob violence (see the 1935 summer attacks on Noyes Academy in Canaan, New Hampshire, for just one example, where white mobs literally dismantled the school using a team of oxen to raze it to the ground).

Conversely in other regions, Baltimore for example, Black schools were effectively ignored by the white population, as educated slaves were a boon to their white owners who profited from a slave's ability to read, write, and perform rudimentary mathematics. These educated Black people could not be seen as the same type of threat to white laborers that was imagined in the North because, simply put, even educated Black labor benefited whiteness and resulted in more valuable property rather than potential Black citizens. As Moss (2010) demonstrates in her thorough analysis of Black citizenship and schooling in antebellum America, there was a trade-off between access to civil rights and access to literacy, with it being near impossible to obtain both.

The Port Royal Experiment (1862–1865)

Immediately after the start of the Civil War, President Lincoln ordered a blockade on all Confederate ports, a move meant to devastate the southern economy by preventing international trade. Seven months into the war, in November 1861, the Battle of Port Royal gave Lincoln a political win and a desperately needed morale boost to Union troops. Relatively unguarded, with only two forts on either side, Port Royal would prove an easy win for the Union and provide a base for its navy, giving them control of waterways between the North and South as well as control over international commerce.

Upon the Union's seizure of the land, nearly every white resident regardless of social class abandoned their homes and their land leaving behind close to 10,000 slaves. Although they became de facto "freedmen," abandoned slaves were officially claimed as "contrabands of war" by Union Major General Benjamin Franklin Butler under Lincoln's command. It is important to highlight here that seemingly freed Black people in this moment remained seized property, to counter the contemporary and reductive claims that "Lincoln freed the slaves"; to be clear, Lincoln's war was a fight for the preservation of the Union, and not for the freedom or humanity of enslaved people.

By the following month, the US secretary of the treasury tasked Edward Pierce, a Union soldier and supervisor of "contraband populations" in Hampton, Virginia, with evaluating and reporting back on the situation in the newly occupied Port Royal and the surrounding islands. Two months later he returned to Washington with a report and a plan to reap the economic benefits of the cotton crops and unlimited laborers for Lincoln's Union, as well as a less enthusiastically received plan for integrating the now (potentially) free Black southerners into the United States through education. The federal government gave Pierce the permission he needed, but not the funding. For that he would have to rely on northerners with a track record of religious fervor and an insatiable work ethic toward salvation of nonwhite peoples across the globe. By early March of 1862 he was given full charge of the land and the people of the Sea Islands, recruiting 53 teachers and superintendents funded by the AMA, Boston's Educational Commissions, New York's Freedmen's Relief Association, and Philadelphia's Port Royal Relief Committee, of which Laura Towne was a member (United

States Department of The Treasury & Pierce, 1862). Missionaries promptly traveled south, moving into abandoned plantation houses and setting up field hospitals and schools, tasked with civilizing the "The negroes [who] had, in the meantime, been without persons to guide and care for them" once freed from slavery. Pierce's report notes that only one Black-run school (John Milton, under the auspices of the Reverend Doctor Peck) was open prior to his arrival, hinting at a gap that needed filling. Recall, however, that only a handful of weeks had passed between the white flight from the Sea Islands and the formation of the first Black-led school. If contemporaneous events throughout the South serve as any indication, we should assume that large numbers of Black schools would have opened and flourished in the Sea Islands under Black teachers and leaders had Pierce and his missionaries not interfered.

In his subsequent report, published as "The Negroes at Port Royal," Pierce praised the saintlike missionaries to Port Royal declaring,

> There was as high a purpose and devotion among them as in any colony that ever went forth to bear the evangel of civilization ... There were some of whom the world was scarce worthy, and to whom, whether they are among the living or the dead, I delight to pay the tribute of my respect and admiration.

The Port Royal missionaries were, like their predecessors around the globe, beyond heroic: they were indescribably devoted to a degree that the rest of humanity would never measure nor deserve.

Unlike prior missionary excursions to the Pacific, there was a less unified ideal shared among the Port Royal recruits. In a somewhat generational split, the younger recruits understood Black education and emancipation from a highly pragmatic view of the Free Soil Movement – "Free soil, free schools, – free ballot boxes, free representation in state and national" governments. To them, slavery was not so much an ethical or moral issue, but it was instead an economic hindrance getting in the way of national progress, free labor, and laissez-faire capitalism. Older generations' abolitionism was more the result of a moral fervor echoing the Second Great Awakening,[3] founded in a range of beliefs from evangelical to Garrisonian Protestant understandings of slavery as an offense against God (Rose, 1976) rather than an abhorrent and violent institution against humanity. Regardless of their divergent inspirations, missionaries in Port Royal were tasked with bringing "civilization" to the contraband slaves of the Sea Islands during the war as what Rose called "rehearsal for Reconstruction," referring to the similarly doomed project of integrating formerly enslaved Black people into the US body politic. Although missionaries aimed to civilize Black Sea Islanders via education and eventual incorporation into capitalist labor, the government's impetus was an economic one: creating a willing workforce who would continue to grow, harvest, and export cotton to benefit the Union economy.

While the Port Royal Experiment was viewed as an educational success in that it helped establish numerous schools (among them Laura Towne's Penn School), it failed to achieve the economic or social aims demanded by the government. Free Black people chose to harvest food they could eat over crops they could sell for minimal profit, seeing little benefit from or difference between working cotton fields under slavery or capitalism. Confiscated Confederate land and homes, once imagined as the future property of the Black people who cultivated and cared for it, were soon (1863) sold to the highest bidder. Although about 2,000 out of 400,000 acres were bought by Black Sea Islanders, the majority went to white northerners who then allowed Black farmers to farm but not own the land – often the very missionaries who advocated for Black land ownership. After Lincoln's death, much of the confiscated land and property in the South was reinstated to Confederate deserters by the Johnson administration in opposition to Union General William T. Sherman's Special Field Orders No. 15 (January 1865), now colloquially known as the promise of "40 acres and a mule."

Reconstruction (1865–1877)

White landowners, planters, and laborers uniformly rejected the idea of organized public schooling already widespread in the North, preferring to retain authority over and education of children within the family. Freedmen, however, were hungry for emancipatory education by any means necessary, and took full advantage of both northern missionary agencies' desire to fund Black schools, as well as their own newly established rights to participate in state and federal governments toward that end. As James D. Anderson reminds us in his essential book *The Education of Blacks in the South, 1860–1935* (1988), Black southerners are the heroes of their own story when it comes to education and that which grew into the first formalized universal school system in the South. Despite the volumes of missionary writing and government reports to the contrary, "the foundation of the freedmen's educational movement was their self-reliance and deep-seated desire to control and sustain schools for themselves and their children" (p. 5). Northern aid was helpful, but it was Black people themselves who worked against and overturned the anti-school ideology of the white South, and who built at least 500 Black-run southern schools by 1866, just one year after the end of the Civil War. Superintendent of Schools for the Freedmen's Bureau, John W. Alvord, confirmed, "This educational movement among the freedmen has in it a self-sustaining element" (quoted in Anderson, 1988, p. 7); in other words, there was at no time a need for heroic white teachers or school administrators. There was, however, a need for the federal government to control a recently freed population of Black citizens, and there was already a well-established method of missionary indoctrination through education that could meet the needs of the government and its white citizenry in maintaining white supremacy. From this vantage point, we can better understand that the movement toward universal free education in the South was a contradictory project fought, on one hand, for collective emancipation and, on the other, for indoctrination and shoring up capitalism; a battle for external versus internal control over Black lives.

Laura's Light and Love

> The heroism of such a life cannot be told; it is enough to know that it has had a lasting effect upon the people among whom it was lived.
> – Alice N. Lincoln, foreword to *Letters and Diary of Laura M. Towne*

Letters and Diary of Laura M. Towne opens with a foreword that makes it known promptly and indisputably that Laura Towne is a hero whose value can be neither measured nor described. Instead, it is claimed, we must read the very words of the hero herself, to live as she has lived, to walk in her footsteps so we might understand viscerally the impact of her life on the generations of formerly enslaved Africans to whom "her name is loved and honored." As with her missionary sisters across the globe, Towne's letters and diaries construct a story of great personal sacrifice and suffering in the pursuit of her godly duty to bring light and love to "the colored race." Despite the editor's claim that Towne wrote her letters and diaries for no particular purpose and "without a thought of publication," the book opens with its subject quoted as saying she had no choice but to spread her knowledge and service to the proverbial masses. She writes, "I am pushed to it by a sense of duty; for the things going on here ought not to be forgotten, nor lost, as a lesson." Thus, Towne's written declaration of her own heroism and devotion "to a noble cause" of saving a "race of people ... like children set suddenly adrift" post-emancipation enters into and furthers the discursive construction of white female missionaries as wholly benevolent, loving, duty-bound, maternal figures without whom entire races of people would certainly never evolve or, perhaps, even survive.

Laura Matilda Towne was born in Pittsburg, Pennsylvania, in 1825, the youngest of four children. After her mother's death when Laura was only seven years old, she and her siblings were raised by their father and educated in Boston, before finally ending up back in Pennsylvania (Philadelphia) during the height of the Industrial Revolution, the "missionary period" in Hawai'i, massive population expansion, and the US Common School era and its subsequent feminization of the teaching profession. Perhaps most influential in Towne's formative years was the burgeoning abolitionist movement she was exposed to first in Boston, and again upon her return to her home state. There, Towne belonged to the First Unitarian Church of Philadelphia led by abolitionist minister William Henry Furness, a colleague and friend of Boston's most well-known abolitionist, William Lloyd Garrison. Reverend Furness was a fervent abolitionist known for fiercely heated antislavery sermons, not always appreciated by his congregation or his fellow Philadelphians. However, this heat when added to Towne's already smoldering spark for abolition, adventure, and serving her country, ignited a fire that would lead to her lifetime commitment to serving and saving the Black population in the newly freed Sea Islands of South Carolina.

As was common with most other missionary women during the 19th century, Towne had already established herself as part of the moral high ground, both through her study of homeopathic medicine and her experience teaching in "charity schools" focused on imparting Christian morals and values to the dramatically expanding population of immigrants and poor in New England. She was already keen on spending her life doing something heroic and meaningful in service to the Union, a more noble cause than what her Philadelphia life was offering. That thirst for adventure and heroism was met in April 1862 in the government's call for northern volunteers to "take charge of the negroes" in Port Royal, and Towne was one of the first women to step forward.

Just weeks shy of her 37th birthday when she arrived in the Sea Islands, Towne was significantly older than the average single woman at the beginning of a missionary journey. She was not able to teach straightaway, but instead spent her early days at the former Pope's Plantation on St. Helena Island satisfied to "keep house" or "do copying or be a kind of clerk to Mr. Pierce, and to be inspector of the huts … [and] inculcating gardens" (Towne, 1912, pp. 12–13). She also distributed clothing and rations, and provided medical care to the residents of the islands. Her diaries and letters make clear, however, that she was destined for something greater, and within her first week in St. Helena she wrote to her sister Rosie that she had plans to "go somewhere else" if she could not in her current posting "do what [she] came for in this position, that is, influence the negroes directly."

Towne's collected letters and diaries, like the other women highlighted in this book, are overflowing with evidence that her purpose as an abolitionist and missionary was more about her own empowerment, her duty to the Union, and her deeply held sense of a precise and singular type of proper moral character and industriousness that only she could pass on to the no longer enslaved residents of the Sea Islands. Along with more mundane recitations of her daily life, her letters and diaries offer a well-illustrated picture of her humble, but self-appointed, heroism, her charmingly dehumanizing view of Black people, and either critique or high praise of her fellow northerners depending on whether they were doing something that she thought she could do better.

From her first St. Helena entry, Towne recounts a story of meeting "two women of colored aristocracy," an initial encounter than affirmed her belief that she was "doing here what no one else could do as well" (Holland, p. 8). As the islands were only very recently freed from their confederate residents, slaveholders and commoners alike, there was understandably strong anxiety among those left behind that their former masters might return at any moment, revoking their newfound freedom and punishing them severely. Towne returns to this theme throughout her writings, as the war and the years pass. Though it is often mentioned that the freedmen ask to go north with the missionaries should the "Secesh" (secessionists) return, Towne and her white colleagues remain prepared to evacuate at any time, however without inclusion of the freedmen though they expressed sadness and concern for their well-being. In other words, it remained clear for years that should the Confederates return to the islands, either as part of a military action or as residents returning to reclaim what was theirs, the white missionaries were prepared to abandon their Black students and neighbors despite somehow remaining their saviors. In reflecting on the freedmen's fear of the confederates' return and deadly retribution, Towne repeatedly describes how white women – herself in particular – served a very specific role in providing calm reassurance to the seemingly inappropriately anxious Black population of Sea Islanders. From her first account with the Black "aristocracy," who she recalls begged her to stay saying, "they could n't be happy widout white ladies 'round'" to being sent around to neighboring plantations to "cheer up and reassure the rather downhearted negroes, or rather the negro women," Towne makes clear to her readers that white women are the true protectors of the freed Black population of the Sea Islands. She notes that this task doesn't cheer her, however, though it is "gratifying to be so able to give comfort. [Black women] think a white lady a great safeguard from danger, and they say they are 'confused' if there are no ladies about" (Towne, 1912, p. 21). Although this is Towne quoting someone else, so perhaps with room for misinterpretation, it is interesting to note that both Towne and the Black women in question understand the protective power held by white women. Bear in mind, the Sea Islands at this time were surrounded by audible gun battles and an ongoing risk of Confederate attack, and yet Towne recounts several interactions during which either she or the women she quotes make clear that white women are "a safeguard from danger" and that "The sight of [white] ladies gives them a feeling of security that nothing else does" (p. 21). While whiteness, and female whiteness in particular, is a protective power in the United States, it is generally understood to protect white women themselves, often at the expense of Black men. However, Towne's recitation of the power of white womanhood is instructive in that she repeatedly reinforces the idea that it is a power that she could radiate out toward others, protecting even Black people under attack by their former owners. Of course, there is some contradiction here, or perhaps more of a moral issue at hand, in that her power as such remains discursive and hypothetical since she seems certain that she would flee the islands at a moment's notice should any real danger arise.

As pointed out throughout this book, it is important we understand the power of Towne's written words as something much more than one individual woman's private diaries or letters home. Missionary women (and men) were required to keep extensive written records in the form of letters (to family, funders, and church) and private journals. Many of them additionally hand-copied their letters home into a bound journal prior to mailing. These writings were widely read by white contemporaries during the 19th century as their key texts in understanding "savage" peoples around the globe. They also assisted in constructing an understanding of Black humanity and potential citizenship, and imagining their own futures living among Black people in a post-emancipation United States. Further, letters written to funders, missionary associations, government officials, and so on were meant to influence policy just as much as they were meant to solicit funding or simply report back on their missions. Towne acknowledges awareness that her letters are read in this manner, noting that they have been read "to committees" in Philadelphia, and have been printed and copied into reports sent to Washington. As such, it is important to re-read these works with a focus on white supremacy, and particularly a gendered analysis of white supremacy, and how that is maintained through the seemingly benign, benevolent actions of empowered white women. Through such a lens, we can adjust the dominant discourse on the history of abolition, the Civil War, and the education of Black children in the United States, as well as our collective conception of the roles of white women in the United States' imperial project abroad and reconstruction at home, and more generally in schooling children of color throughout history and into the present day.

Additionally significant to the persistence of the discursive power of 19th-century women's confessional literature is the power held in real time over the freedmen in particularly subtle ways by white women. The calming effect of white women on the freedmen is used to specifically pacify and convince freedmen to continue working the valuable cotton fields in the Sea Islands, this time for capitalism and Uncle Sam rather than for white masters. Towne calls this level of influence "a triumph, after having been rejected as useless" (Towne, 1912, p. 26), describing the empowerment she feels from convincing Black people to work cotton fields against their wishes for what she admits is an unfair wage of one dollar per acre. Moreover, she acknowledges that the freedmen prefer to work the crops that provided actual sustenance for their families – corn, primarily – rather than harvesting cotton and being paid in banknotes, which to them were unrecognizable and thus have no value. Towne does not merely acknowledge this forced labor or her power within it, she finds humor in it. Knowing that the main goal of the Port Royal Experiment is to demonstrate that free Black people would work cotton fields under capitalism as productively as they did under the lash, Towne laments only that some supervisors have merely "changed the mode of compulsion" from whipping to "holding a tyrant's power over them" (Towne, 1912, p. 55). She then writes in her diary that the proper way to earn obedience is through earning the field workers' love. Extolling her own success at saving the people she "found" she describes them just two months after her arrival as "jolly and happy and decently fed and dressed, and so full of affection and gratitude to the people who are relieving them that it is rather too flattering to be enjoyed." This happiness and joy are the result of missionary love and care and "is genuine now and they are working like Trojans." She continues, with a clear misunderstanding of what abolition means, "It is such a satisfaction to an abolitionist to see that they [freedmen] are proving conclusively that they can and will and even like to work enough at least to support themselves and give something extra to Government" (p. 68). Yet she acknowledges that this work is not done by choice, but by the combined force of white men threatening to destroy Black corn crops and white women using their maternal power to influence and "calm" the freedmen into submission.

The irony and importance of her critiquing some white men's "holding power" over the freedmen while she uses her own feminized power to do the same should not be lost on us. This conflation of love, fear, and power is a constant refrain throughout Towne's diaries and letters. She writes more about how loved and respected Pierce is than she comments on her own sense of being loved; that is to say, she names the feelings directed at Pierce as love explicitly, whereas she refers to the emotions she evokes as appreciation, comfort, and feeling safeguarded – maternal incarnations of the same emotions. Regardless of gendered word choice, Towne conflates freedmen's obedience and kind words while experiencing fear for their lives as evidence of love, despite the power dynamics at play. Yet Towne writes in both her diary and letters home that she finds it "touching" to "hear negroes begging Mr. Pierce to let them plant and tend corn and not cotton," agreeing with another supervisor, Mr. Philbrick, that they are "docile generally and require the positive ordering that children of five or ten years of age require" and that they are indeed afraid of any white man, Yankee or Confederate.

Such infantilization and dehumanization of Black adults and children is a common trope throughout Towne's writings. In her first week on St. Helena, she writes home,

> The number of little darkies tumbling about at all hours is marvellous [*sic*]. They swarm on the front porch and in the front hall. If a carriage stops it is instantly surrounded by a dozen or more woolly heads. They are all very civil, but full of mischief and fun.
>
> (Towne, 1912, p. 11)

She years later describes her growing collection of dogs in the same manner. The conflation is so severe, in fact, that it is difficult to discern when reading her texts whether she is referring to animals or humans, specifically when she calls her subjects the diminutive "pet." In a letter dated July 17, 1862, Towne writes,

> We had the prettiest little baby born here the other day that I ever saw, and good as gold. It is a great pet with us all. Indeed, it is almost laughable to see what pets all the people are and how they enjoy it.

Years later, despite living among the freedmen and claiming to see them as "her own people," she continues the practice of referring to Black people as her pets and using animalizing tropes. In a letter dated March 9, 1866, she sends photos home, writing, "I send the enclosed picture of me with three of my pets," referring to what we soon discover are actually three Black human beings. One is described as a young man who is "incorrigibly slow and stupid," while the other two girls are considered bright in some regard, but "very dull and slow" in others. They are indeed her pets, treated as such, and for whom her "face is burnt out so as to do justice to them" (Towne, 1912, p. 172).

Other Black neighbors she expresses love and care for are likewise described as a "dumb brute" with a "dogged countenance [that] shows why he was so whipped" (176), or via physical description similar to those she uses to describe her dogs and horses – strong build, brand shoulders, hard worker, "little darkies" who are "large and strong" girls (182), "about the worst little monkey that ever was" (p. 219), and so on. To Towne, pets are any manner of nonhuman entities under her care, including plants, calves, a Black boy she hopes to give away to friends up north, and a dog named Tim, among countless others. Speaking literally about her own pet dogs (letter dated June 24, 1877), Towne speaks more lovingly than she has spoken about her pet freedmen, but reading through her written words and between the lines, we cannot miss the metaphor that helps understand her view of Black people and their role in her own spiritual and moral fulfillment:

> Pets give us grief as well as comfort and pleasure, but I think the latter greatly counterbalances, and besides, I think we ought to take some pets to our hearts and homes to ameliorate the condition of something in the world.

This is not unlike her explanation for her missionary work and identifying with the abolitionist movement: she must ameliorate the condition of the world, not necessarily the condition of enslaved humans, and she must do so at great personal sacrifice. From her early mention of the sacrifice of leaving her family – which harms her family more so than it does her, to the sacrifice she mentions in sending a letter home via steamer rather than traveling to visit for the holidays herself, Towne's words echoes Hawaiian missionaries before her (see Chapter 2) in the repeated description of suffering in the name of others' salvation that is both by choice and somehow also out of her hands, claiming her sacrifice is not by "free will, but by really cruel circumstance" that leave her "bitterly disappointed" as well.

As was also common among 19th-century missionary women, and a key reason why they generally came from moneyed families, Towne rarely took a salary during her decades teaching in the Sea Islands. By September 1865, just over three years into her tour of duty, Towne notes she was "just contemplating taking a salary." She then narrates one of several "Sophie's Choice" moments, contemplating whether to take a salary more than once offered her which, if accepted, will taint her otherwise saintly implicit vow of poverty, her way of thinking of herself and her role in Black salvation, and the way she has been seen as getting "credit for being a volunteer, all over the county." She further laments,

> If I could only afford to live without, I am sure it would be best policy, as well as best pleasure, to do it. But can I? … I suppose I must take for granted my inability to do without it, and so take the salary, for by all that I know of my means, this is the case.
>
> (pp. 165–166)

Within a year, when northern aid for Black schools was scarce as Reconstruction dwindled to an end, Towne gave up her salary once again "so that the school may go on as it is for one or two years longer" (p. 242). She narrates a series of communications between herself and Francis R. Cope of Philadelphia, financial agent for the Penn School, in which her sacrifice and suffering are made clear. Yet Towne also notes that it is her brother's "liberal" financial backing that allows her to make these sacrifices; whenever she reached out for his support "he answered, saying he had no doubt I took great pleasure in this arrangement, as I enjoyed before being a volunteer teacher so much, and apparently he was very glad to have the Fund spun out longer" (Towne, 1912, p. 242). At a later event, Towne shares that the people were told "that I was teaching for nothing, and so was Ellen, so we were duly glorified and abashed" (p. 266). To live without a salary brought glory and suffering; to accept a salary is just a different kind of glory and suffering. Either way, the sacrifice must be made for to uplift the "negro race," and thus also to rebuild the Union.

What is different about Towne, and is thus quite instructive, is the way she removes herself from identification with the "bad whites" with whom she groups not only the secessionists and slaveholders, but the other white women teachers as well. While it is expected to hear a self-described abolitionist critique the Confederates, slavery, northerners who support slavery, and so on, Towne lets slip a persistent idea of being – to use a term anachronistically – more woke than the other white women teachers. Within a month of having arrived in St. Helena, Towne had the opportunity to teach in place of Miss Ware who was out sick, a position for which she had already expressed great envy. In a lengthy diary entry dated May 4, 1862, "the day after my thirty-seventh birthday," she evaluates her performance quite highly, and notes that she found another teacher "with a long switch whipping two of the girls." Towne intervened, telling teacher, "I had come here to stop whipping, not to inflict it" (Holland, p. 38), echoing her ongoing critique of the best way to convince Black laborers to work cotton fields was through love rather than through the lash.

And yet Towne's apparent abhorrence of whipping as a pedagogical method is inconsistently enforced outside of her own local sphere of influence, even after she is named superintendent of the Philadelphia schools and "agent for the Pennsylvania Freedmen's Relief Association down here" (March 1865). In her role as superintendent, she witnesses poor quality teaching and mistreatment of students, yet doesn't interfere. She does, however, make clear that she is of a different breed of white teacher than those she critiques. At a church event she meets "two southern teachers" who she describes as "tawdrily dressed" and "undoubted rebels" during the war, writing,

> we hear that they whip the children in their school and make them call them 'massa' and 'missus,' as in the old time. But they are 'nigger teachers,' so I did my duty by them as agreeably as I could. They send their reports regularly, and so do their duty by me.
>
> (Towne, 1912, p. 179)

Towne's expressed superiority to the other schools and their white teachers repeats throughout her diaries. In March 1863, when she finally has her own school, she reflects on a visit from Mr. Pierce during which her students per-formed impressively, answering his questions "pretty readily." That night she "had a long talk with him about Miss Buggies' school," one of several perceived competitors in the race to save the hearts and minds of the Black Sea Islanders and thus create a model to do the same for the entirety of Black America post-emancipation. Towne and her school are better loved, she tells Pierce, noting that Buggies

> complains that the children will not go to her and will come to us. She thinks we ought to forbid them. We maintain that they were our scholars long before she came down here, that they are attached to us and we to them.
>
> (Towne, 1912, p. 108)

Even once her school enrollment grew to an unmanageable size, making her unable to hear students over the sounds of the other classes happening simulta-neously in the same room, Towne appears committed to being the sole white woman "doing here what no one else could do as well" (p. 8) through her ability to "influence the negroes directly" (p. 14). Over a decade later, her diaries and letters express the same sentiment: her school is "a delight" and a gift to the com-munity. There is nowhere else her students would rather be, and "to be deprived of a lesson is severe punishment." Based upon her teaching, she is as confident as ever that "this race is going to rise. It is biding its time" (Towne, 1912, p. 281). She is a hero among other white women, the "good white" despite the many ways in which she is inflicting racist violence, reinforcing unpaid or low-wage labor, and impeding true emancipation and the exercise of free will among the not-quite-free freedmen.

What is especially intriguing about this discourse is the way it foreshadows the 21st-century benevolent whiteness that inundates our contemporary educational system and those teachers who continue to write about their roles within it. There remains a persistent sense of benevolence embodied by "good white teachers" who earn that self-appointed moniker by calling out the more visibly racist behaviors of their peers. This in turn buys the "good white teachers" a pass and frees them from agency or accountability in reproducing systemic white supremacy in schools. In Towne's case, in addition to the ways in which she reinforces the white supremacist racial order through benevolent whiteness as a pseudo loving act, through using her maternal role to encourage forced low-wage labor in service of the capitalist state or through her infantilization of Black adults and animalization of her Black students and "pets," it is imperative that we pay attention to the way in which she reproduces directly and indirectly white supremacy through replacing and preventing the establishment of Black-led schools, a persistent act of benevolent whiteness in contemporary times as well.

Conclusion

I close this chapter by returning to the plea put forth by Rupert Holland in his preface to the published *Letters and Diaries of Laura Towne*, that we "must read between the lines to complete the picture." Towne's work – her teaching as well as her collected writings – makes visible in its narratives and its omissions one important piece of information: Black education in the South existed long before Towne's heroic arrival in the Sea Islands. Although the quantity and quality, as well as the legality of Black-led schools varied across time and geography in the 19th-century United States, there is overwhelming evidence that Black schooling was everywhere, and it was valued beyond measure as the key to an entire people's emancipation. While Towne dedicates just one diary entry (Monday, April 28, 1862) to Black schools in St. Helena prior to her arrival, referring to Will Capers and his "secret night school for men" (p. 27), we must assume that his was not the only school closed upon the commencement of the Port Royal Experiment, nor would it have been the last.

We must remember that Black education always already existed in the South, both antebellum and post-emancipation. There was no need for the performative heroism of northern whites to bring their own methods of education to the masses. Education for emancipation existed in Black communities long before the prospect of government-mandated emancipation was imaginable. There are countless Black scholars who have for decades written libraries full of this history and whose works on the subject should be widely read for an in-depth understanding of Black educational history to which I cannot do justice in the limited scope of this chapter. Frederick Douglass, W.E.B. DuBois, and Booker T.

Washington are perhaps the most well-known Black scholars on the subject, and as such are often the beginning and end of the recital of Black educational history. With too many to list here, I recommend for starters a complete reading of the texts cited in this chapter, including Anderson's (1988) *The Education of Blacks in the South, 1860–1935*, Butchart's (2010) *Schooling the Freed People: Teaching, Learning, and the Struggle for Black Freedom, 1861–1876*, Jones's (1980) *Soldiers of Light and Love: Northern Teachers and Georgia Blacks, 1865–1873*, and Moss's (2010) *Schooling Citizens: The Struggle for African American Education in Antebellum America*. In addition, required reading for all educators and educational scholars alike must include my colleague and former classmate Jarvis Givens's *Fugitive Pedagogy: Carter G. Woodson and the Art of Black Teaching*, just released as I finalized my own manuscript.

I name these texts here in the body of this chapter rather than as a footnote to highlight their existence and relevance, as an explicitly political choice to amplify the already existing voices on Black education in the United States whose work must be understood as the intellectual ground upon which I stand in developing my own theorization of benevolent whiteness in the education of Black and Indigenous students. While this book centers the stories of white womanhood, it does so to highlight whiteness as not something normalized or heroic, but as persistently violent and influential in the formation and ongoing legacy of schooling in the United States. Rather than telling the history of Black education in depth, the focus of this book is to refuse the narrative that missionary teachers in the postwar South were inherently heroic or that schools and schooling needed to be brought to a place where in fact those things had a rich history. It seeks to make visible the more benevolently violent inspirations behind the massive missionary influx to the South during and after the Civil War, and again delineates the ways in which benevolent whiteness reinforces white supremacy, ideologically and subtly, through the feminized and loving role of missionary women teachers. Taken in conversation with the histories of Black-led education, this chapter highlights the importance of understanding the difference between authentic loving desires behind education for emancipation versus the falsely "loving desires" of benevolent whiteness at play in education for Americanization, indoctrination, capitalism, and white supremacy. In other words, this chapter intends to make visible the difference between education as a tool for gaining control over a people's own future versus as a tool for controlling a people.

As the latter, we must understand the deployment of white women teachers as the ideological arm of anti-Blackness and as the counterpart to the more recognizably violent white male military troops enforcing the same ideology. Such an understanding of the genealogy of schooling in the United States, and a desire to imagine schooling's decolonized futures, require a nuanced understanding of the relationships between settler colonialism and anti-Blackness and the roles schools and teachers have played in supporting those structures. It also makes visible in the ruptures and erasures how Black and Indigenous communities have historically and contemporarily always created spaces of resistance and solidarity. Toward this end, educational scholars, teachers, school leaders, and community members of color along with white accomplices are compelled and positioned to break free from the violent trappings of settler colonialism and anti-Blackness and bring forth multiple new educational futurities.

Notes

1 Samuel Chapman Armstrong. (n.d.). Retrieved December 3, 2016, from http://www.hamptonu.edu/about/armstrong.cfm.
2 For an excellent exploration of the complexity of Black education in the prewar United States, see Moss (2010). *Schooling citizens: The struggle for African American education in antebellum America.*
3 See Chapter 1 for a more in-depth discussion of the Second Great Awakening.

References

Anderson, J. D. (1988). *The education of Blacks in the South, 1860–1935.* Chapel Hill: University of North Carolina Press.

Butchart, R. E. (2010). *Schooling the freed people: Teaching, learning, and the struggle for black freedom, 1861–1876.* University of North Carolina Press.

Hampton Institute. (1893). *Twenty-two years' work of the Hampton Normal and Agricultural Institute at Hampton, Virginia: Records of Negro and Indian graduates and ex-students, with historical and personal sketches and testimony on important race questions from within and without; to which are added ... some of the songs of the races gathered in the school.* Hampton: Normal School Press.

Jones, J. (1980). *Soldiers of light and love: Northern teachers and Georgia blacks, 1865–1873.* Chapel Hill: University of North Carolina Press.

Leonardo, Z., & Boas, E. (2013). Other kids' teachers: What children of color learn from white women and what this says about race, whiteness, and gender. In Marvin Lynn, & Adrienne D. Dixson (eds.), *Handbook of Critical Race Theory in Education*, 313–324.

Moss, H. J. (2010). *Schooling citizens: The struggle for African American education in antebellum America.* Chicago: University of Chicago Press.

Rose, W. L. (1976). *Rehearsal for reconstruction: the Port Royal experiment.* New York, NY: Oxford University Press.

Towne, L. M. (1912). In Holland, R. S., & Cairns Collection of American Women Writers *Letters and diary of Laura M. Towne: Written from the Sea islands of South Carolina, 1862–1884.* Cambridge, MA: Printed at the Riverside Press.

United States Department of The Treasury & Pierce, E. L. (1862). The negroes at Port Royal. Report of E. L. Pierce, government agent, to the Hon. Salmon P. Chase, secretary of the Treasury. Boston, R. F. Wallcut. [Web.] Retrieved from the Library of Congress, https://lccn.loc.gov/12001839

4

SISTER TO THE SIOUX

Elaine Goodale Eastman

> If there is an idol that the American people have, it is the school ... It is a remedy
> for barbarism we think, so we give them the dose. Uncle Sam is like a man set-
> ting a charge of powder. The school is the slow match. He lights it and goes off
> whistling, sure that in time it will blow up the old life, and of its shattered pieces
> he will make good citizens.
>
>   – Annie Beecher Scoville, missionary to the Sioux, 1901

In this chapter, I turn toward the role of white womanhood and benevolent
whiteness as constructed in Native American Indian boarding schools. This
chapter is again framed within the social and political contexts of the time and
traces the circuit of benevolent whiteness as it travels back to its roots, often
by way of missionary descendants who took what they learned in Hawai'i and
applied it unilaterally toward the education of Indigenous peoples (and emancipated Black people) on the continent. As in the previous chapter, I ask readers
to consider how we can view 19th-century women's diaries and journals – their
"truths" – through a lens that clarifies the history of teaching and schools as sites
of settler colonialism, its related violence, and the gendered power dynamics
traditionally normalized or made invisible by the very women in power. This
complicates the narrative that white women in the 19th century were entirely
without agency and were themselves only victims of patriarchy and thus *unwilling* participants in the violence required for US imperial expansion. By tracing
and analyzing the repeated recitations of love and benevolence found in these
women's letters and diaries, this chapter asks readers to consider what it means
when "good intentions" produce malevolent results, and, more importantly, why
we insist collectively that good intentions excuse negative outcomes. How can
we decouple "good intentions" from the structural, ideological, physical, and
material violence that so often result from benevolent whiteness and its loving

DOI: 10.4324/9781003201809-5

intentions? Who determines what intentions are good in the first place? After all, colonialism was benevolent in the eyes of the colonizer state, as were missions in the minds of missionaries, regardless of their genocidal effects on Indigenous peoples, colonized tribal nations, and enslaved Africans.

During the early decades of the 19th century, white women inspired by the Second Great Awakening[1] found the Protestant foreign missionary cause an avenue through which to access agency and adventure in an otherwise male-dominated culture. A half century later, US patriarchy continued to bar women from political, business, and most professional pursuits. However, white women of the 1880s like Elaine Goodale (1863–1953) had the Indian Reform Movement, a campaign to assimilate Indians[2] in response to the "Indian Problem."[3] While the self-appointed "reformers" included men and women, predominantly "white, eastern, urban, Protestant, well-educated and well-off" (Bannan, 1978, p. 787) women took up the on-the-ground work of reforming "savages" toward "civilization" in the now-feminized profession of teaching. During the period immediately following the Reconstruction era, teaching was completely feminized and structured around Horace Mann's "common schools" movement,[4] while the demand for teachers was at the highest of any time in the country's history. By the 1880s, the teaching profession was between two-thirds and three-quarters occupied by women depending on location, and schooling was (as in colonial outposts) the method through which white missionaries and the US government would attempt to "Americanize" and disenfranchise Indigenous peoples. Empowered and funded by the 1819 Indian Civilization Act and the Bureau of Indian Affairs, individuals and religious groups made it their mission to teach and live among the Indians (in reservations and boarding schools) with the goal of complete Indian assimilation into whiteness. Elaine Goodale Eastman was perhaps the most powerful woman involved in this project.

Background: Social and Political Context

To understand the context within which a woman garnered freedom and power in an otherwise anti-woman society, it is necessary to first look at the events of the earlier 19th century. Although the US government had complex and ongoing relationships with Indigenous tribes from the moment a formal US state existed, I begin my historical chronology in the early 19th century for several reasons, most importantly because this is the time in our country's history during which "Americanization" through schooling became formally organized as a means of assimilating or colonizing nonwhite peoples across the globe. Additionally, the second and third decades of the 19th century mark, respectively, the Missionary Period in Hawai'i and the beginning of the common school movement, as well as the commonly accepted beginning of formalized Indian education in the United States. Therefore, bounding this chapter within roughly the same time frame as the previous two serves to provide an overall picture of the intentional organization of schooling as a tool of Americanization and white supremacy.

On March 3, 1819, Congress passed the Indian Civilization Fund Act "for the purpose of providing against the further decline and final extinction of the Indian tribes, adjoining the frontier settlements of the United States, and for introducing among them the habits and arts of civilization ... to employ capable persons of good moral character [to teach Indian adults and children]."[5] The act approved an annual sum of $10,000 for any religious groups or individuals who chose to teach and live among the Indians, resulting in the creation of missionary schools on and off Indian reservations. Despite the seemingly benevolent claim of preventing further decline and extinction of Indian tribes, the true purpose of the Act was effectively the opposite: to exterminate Indian culture and identity through systematic assimilation into 19th-century American white culture. Fueled by capitalist desire and the sense of moral necessity resulting from the Second Great Awakening, white middle-class Americans felt a moral and patriotic duty to assimilate Indians into Christianity, permanent agricultural[6] (as opposed to nomadic hunting) lifestyles involving ownership of private property, an "Americanized" understanding of citizenship and democracy, and the Protestant work ethic and gender and familial roles. Missionary and Superintendent of Indian Trade/Affairs (1816–1830) Thomas McKenney was a strong believer in the potential for social control and civilization by way of organized schooling, greatly inspired by the work of the American Board of Commissioners for Foreign Missions (ABCFM). His main aim in (successfully) urging missionaries to petition Congress to pass the act was to fund missionary-led schools to test his hypothesis that schooling could turn savages into civilized Christian Americans within just one generation (Keller, 2000; Spring, 2016).

In January of 1824, the secretary of war, John C. Calhoun, a staunch supporter of slavery and southern separatism, unilaterally created the Bureau of Indian Affairs (BIA)[7] in the War Department.[8] Although the wording used in the department's founding stated it was meant to oversee the federal government trade and treaty relations, the primary purpose of the bureau was to administer the McKenney's Indian Civilization Fund,[9] dividing it among Christian missionary groups with the primary purpose of establishing (or strengthening and aligning already operating) schools with approved plans for educating Indigenous children in gender-specific agricultural and domestic skills. Calhoun named McKenney head of the BIA and within three months 21 Indian schools were operating with federal funding, more than fulfilling McKenney's vision. McKenney's belief in the civilizing potential of schools for Native Americans was short-lived, however, and after a tour of "Indian Country" in late 1827 he formally urged Congress to pass an Indian Removal bill.

The 1829 discovery of gold in Cherokee territory, along with the ever-increasing demands and illegal attempts by white settlers to acquire Indian land, led to heightened governmental impatience with the failed plan for Indian erasure by way of assimilation. On May 28, 1830, President Andrew Jackson signed the Indian Removal Act authorizing the president to grant tribes land west of the Mississippi (recently acquired through the Louisiana Purchase) in return for their fertile and resource-rich lands east of the Mississippi. Although Jackson was the first to sign into law Indian removal, the stage was set for nearly three decades prior, beginning with Thomas Jefferson's Indian policy, which aimed to free up Indigenous land for white settlers and to facilitate trade as a means of keeping tribes allied with the United States rather than European colonizers (England and Spain) in North America (Keller, 2000, p. 42). During the 1830s, the Indigenous population east of the Mississippi dwindled to near-uncountable lows: some tribes went willingly, in exchange for money, land, and what they viewed as the potential lesser evil; many resisted, resulting in a series of battles and wars between Native tribes and the US government.

In 1831 the Choctaw were the first tribe to be completely removed from their land under threat of invasion by the US Army, followed by the Creek tribe in 1832, with thousands of each tribe dying during the journey on the "Trail of Tears." The Cherokee were a more divided tribe, with some members willing to accept payment for their land, while others demanded to stay and fight. In 1835, a small group of self-appointed Cherokee representatives agreed to sell their land, and despite the refusal of such a treaty by nearly 16,000 members of the tribe, the government considered the sale a done deal. Over the next three years, only a small fraction of the Cherokee Nation had moved west (approximately 2,000), fueling the government's ire. During the fall and winter of 1838 and 1839, on President Van Buren's orders, the US Army forcibly removed the Cherokee from their land (and their gold) relocating them by foot over 1,200 miles to present-day Oklahoma, despite the fact that the Supreme Court (Worcester v. Georgia, 31 U.S. 515, 1832) expressly prohibited the president's authority to do so.

Common Schools and Americanization (1837–1880)

As with missionary education in Hawai'i, the educational "reform"[10] move-ment in the continental United States was merely a standardization of whiteness as American identity for those who could be easily absorbed into it (western European immigrants), and a means by which to get Indigenous peoples as close to whiteness (or away from Indigenous legitimacy) as possible to effectively eradicate them. In short, education was the clichéd "melting pot" praised in contemporary false nostalgia, but with a far more malevolent purpose than we have been led to believe.

Nineteenth-century education reformers in Massachusetts, led by the "father of common schools," Horace Mann, led a movement toward establishing "com-mon schools" supported by tax dollars and which anyone could attend – provided they were white and male.[11] Responding to the expansion in white male suf-frage (via the removal of the property requirement for voting), industrialization, urbanization, and an increase in immigration, educational reformers argued that common schools could do the work unfit mothers (generally either poor white or nonwhite mothers) could not: creating good citizens and thereby uniting society, and decreasing crime and poverty (Katznelson & Weir, 1988). By the end of the 19th century, free public elementary education was available for most white children in New England regardless of gender. For white, or white-adjacent, students, common schools served as sites for Americanization through basic literacy and numeracy skills and the building of a white Protestant identity, preparing this class of citizens for its proper place on the societal and economic ladder (Tyack, 2003). Meanwhile, wealthy families continued to employ private tutors or send their children to private preparatory schools with classical academic curriculum. As discussed in Chapter 2, the common schools movement coincided with the feminization of teaching, and by the 1880s schools and teaching were ideologically and structurally defined to reflect the values of both movements.

Meant to teach a "common" body of knowledge that would give everyone the same opportunities, Horace Mann's model schools soon spread to other states and the idea of universal American schooling was born. He argued that creating a public that possessed a rudimentary level of literacy and a shared set of core beliefs could best ensure American sociopolitical stability. He claimed, "A republican form of government, without intelligence in the people, must be, on a vast scale, what a mad-house, without superintendent or keepers, would be on a small one" (Mann, 1848).

Despite Mann's call for all children to learn together in "common" schools, he never took a stand against school segregation in his own city. As with other policies rhetorically aimed at "all" Americans, school policy for "all" children in the Progressive era was commonly understood and interpreted to mean all white Americans (and, by necessity, all near-white immigrants). Americanization, then, was synonymous with "white-ification" – a welcoming into the fold of whiteness to those who had previously not been considered "pure" enough to assimilate into the white race. This did not go as far as to include Asians, Native Americans, and certainly not Blacks, but those who could add to the numbers of whites in a country increasingly less white were welcome with the caveat that they must forsake all else aside from their new American identity:

> a self-conscious effort was made to define the Anglo-American or American identity and to defend it as the product of a melting pot assimilationism, and not simply as the maintenance of one group's dominance, while deliberately controlling who was to be eligible to assimilate. This identity was used politically in the Americanization Movement.
>
> (King, 2000, p. 86)

From the outset, the role of schools was to construct discursively a white American identity, to "provide a common language and narrative of the history of the United States" (King, 2000, p. 89). What is clear is that common schools were meant not necessarily to create a literate and educated populace for the sake of an elevated humanity, although that is the romanticized false-memory often employed when invoking Mann's legacy; rather, the goal of schools was a massive indoctrination in ideological whiteness and Americanization during a time of great upheaval – massive immigration, a world war, and a growing population of urban poor. As in the ideological colonization of the Hawaiian Kingdom, continental American statesmen knew that education was the fastest, most far-reaching method of hegemonic domination and thus the most efficient manner of Americanizing the waves of recent European immigrants pouring into the United States. Proponents and directors of common schools proudly proselytized that "the public schools are the biggest Americanizing agency in the United States – they have been ever since we have had public schools" (King, 2000, p. 88).

Black Education, Pre– and Post–Civil War (1830s–1880s)

Because the common school movement began during slavery – roughly 25 years before the start of the Civil War – there was initially no need to consider the organized and federally funded education of enslaved Black children. Unlike the assimilationist education of the near- and newly white, as well as the use of education as a tool for colonizing island nations, the education of Black children (and adults) was seen as a direct threat to white citizenship in most of New England, where educated Blacks were seen as economic competition.[12] Regardless of legal, economic, or political restrictions, free and enslaved Black people did everything in their power to become educated, either formally or in secret. Prior to Nat Turner's Rebellion (1831), there were few laws preventing Black education. Free Black people had organized schools and reading groups for adults and children, while many slave owners allowed or provided for education to their slaves. After the rebellion, southern states made Black education and congregation without a licensed white presence illegal, and it remained so until the South lost the Civil War in 1865 (Anderson, 1988, p. 148).

Post–Civil War, expanding Black literacy was a crucial focus of Black activists and white abolitionists alike. Although key leaders in the Black educational movement (largely Du Bois versus Washington)[13] disagreed on the focus and goals of Black education, there was unanimous agreement among Black and white educators and "reformers" that education was vital to the success of the new free Black citizenry.[14] Despite the reductive story most of us are taught throughout our own schooling experiences, postwar freedom for enslaved Black people simply did not translate to an invitation to public schools, segregated or otherwise. To a great degree, geographic and economic location decided the type of schooling available to Black children (and adults) throughout the United States, as it does into the present day. In the South, many postwar schools had formerly operated as clandestine schools led by members of the Black community. Black men and women opened new schools in record numbers, funded in small part by the federal government and benevolent societies, including the American Missionary Association (AMA), the National Freedmen's Relief Association, and the Freedmen's Bureau, but predominantly sustained by the community itself. The AMA had already established a new missionary outpost, this time at home, providing schooling for salvation in the antebellum south. The primary teachers in AMA common schools, as was the trend across the United States, were white middle-class women from northern states. Once the war ended, the AMA focused on rapidly expanding its educational empire in the south, increasing its teaching corps from 250 to 538 teachers, extending their influence to nearly 70,000 students within a two-year period. During Reconstruction alone, over 3,000 Black schools were established in the South, with a focus on literacy and teacher preparation (Butchart, 1980; Richardson, 2009).

In addition to establishing common schools, the AMA and the Freedman's Bureau provided funding for normal schools (teacher training schools) and colleges in the South, following the standard missionary goals of spreading the gospel tenfold by creating teachers from within colonized societies. Included among the new AMA schools was one of the most well-known: Hampton Normal and Agricultural Institute established in 1868 in Hampton, Virginia. Hampton was founded by Samuel Chapman Armstrong, a Union Army colonel and commander of USCT during the Civil War, and the son of AMA missionaries in Hawai'i. Armstrong's experience commanding the 8th USCT is cited as his first moment of interest in Black welfare. His experience growing up as a member of a missionary family, bearing lifelong witness to the AMA methods of schooling and Christianizing Kanaka Maoli, informed his beliefs in the purposes and possibilities of schooling for Black and (later) Indigenous peoples, stating:

> It meant something to the Hampton School, and perhaps to the ex-slaves of America, that, from 1820 to 1860, the distinctly missionary period, there was worked out in the Hawaiian Islands, the problem of the emancipation, enfranchisement and Christian civilization of a dark-skinned Polynesian people in many respects like the Negro race.
>
> (Hampton Institute, 1893, p. 1)

Following his missionary parents' methods, Armstrong designed Hampton to educate Black children by schooling "the head, the hand, and the heart," training students who would return to their communities to spread AMA ideologies and Christian capitalist beliefs and behavior among their people. To be clear, Armstrong was not the unwavering advocate for Black people's freedom that he is generally made out to be; rather, his goals were to change the Black person to fit the already established order of the South, not to change the realities of an unfair South to benefit Black citizens. His letters demonstrate a feeling only slightly above contempt when it came to Black people as citizens and humans, calling them "worse than the Kanakas, and … hardly worth fighting for."[15] He further clarified his position on "the Negro" in a letter to Archibald Hopkins dated 8 December 1862, writing,

> "I am sort of an abolitionist, but I have not learned to love the Negro. I believe in universal freedom; I believe the whole world cannot buy a single soul … more on account of their souls than their bodies."

Armstrong made it clear, as did most of his abolitionist reform peers, that their fight against slavery was aligned with the Protestant belief in the inability for anyone but God to own a human soul; thus, the institution of slavery was putting the United States and its white citizenry at odds with God Himself.

For both the reformers and the government, the movement for postwar Black education soon inspired extending the cause to include Indian education to further "civilize" nonwhite peoples on the continent just as missionaries were attempting the same abroad. The bulk of the effort toward civilizing Indian children took place in government-funded boarding schools. In 1878, Civil War captain Richard Henry Pratt brought 17 of his Indian prisoners of war to Armstrong's Hampton Normal and Agricultural Institute and began what would grow into their "Indian Department." The following year, The Bureau of Indian Affairs developed the first off-reservation day and boarding schools, including Pratt's now famous Carlisle Indian industrial School in Pennsylvania. Pratt modeled Carlisle after Hampton and aimed to achieve total assimilation of Indians into American whiteness by way of separation from family and culture, indoctrination into the "Protestant work ethic," training in manual labor and agriculture, and complete disavowal of Indigenous customs and culture through his mandate to "kill the Indian in him, and save the man."[16] Carlisle quickly became the model for twenty-six similar Indian boarding schools with the same goal: assimilation through education. Many of the students enrolled in these boarding schools were taken from their homes without parental permission and often by force to a "miserable state of cultural dislocation" (Wu, 2009).

At Hampton, following the national trend, white women taught Black and Indigenous students. The exception to this rule was the teaching of ethics and citizenship, which was either taught by Armstrong himself or by other white men (Anderson, 1988). This is not surprising for the time, given the belief that women could be positively influential only at the primary level, with secondary education and school administration remaining male-dominated fields. Women were seen as inherently motherly, kind, and nurturing, all qualities desired in teaching *younger* children to obey out of obligation and desire for maternal approval. Young, single, middle-class women known for their piety and a desire of selfless service at any cost were eagerly recruited to teach at both residential and on-reservation schools in the hopes that they could create decent, hardworking citizens out of children and parents alike. Leaving home to teach Indigenous students afforded young women more agency and influence than otherwise possible in the 19th century, fulfilling their sense of moral duty as well as their deep yearning for adventure and freedom. One of the most well-known, and most powerful of these missionary mother surrogates was Elaine Goodale Eastman, a young Hampton teacher who in a matter of a few short years ascended to one of the highest offices in public education.

Sister to the Sioux: Elaine Goodale Eastman

Elaine Goodale was born in 1863 during the middle of, yet geographically removed from, the US Civil War. She was the first of four children in a literary-minded, but puritanical, family in the Berkshire Hills of Massachusetts; her father was a teacher and would-be farmer but "Yankee to the backbone," and her mother a pretentious, "city-bred girl," were both descendants of well-known colonial families. Three years later, her younger sister and "constant companion" Dora was born. The two sisters were published and prolific child poets, selling more than 10,000 copies of their first book of poetry. Despite their literary fame, however, the Goodale sisters and their siblings were homeschooled and intentionally isolated from their peers and most of the outside world. They were taught classical curricula of Greek, Latin, art, botany, and literature (with an uncompromising restriction against reading fiction of any kind). Following the evangelical leaning of the time, the Goodale matriarch, Dora Reed Goodale, taught her children to honor duty and service above all else – a refrain that her eldest daughter would cite throughout her life as self-appointed "sister to the Sioux" and hero to Indians in general.

When Elaine was 15, Samuel Chapman Armstrong, founder of the Hampton Institute, visited the Goodale home during one of his many trips to raise funds for the cause of educating and assimilating freedmen. Elaine was instantly as enamored by Armstrong as he was impressed with her intellect and desire to serve selflessly (though at the time she had no real idea how that service would happen). Armstrong remained in touch with the Goodale family, returning for visits often in the coming years. In her diary Elaine notes, "From that hour of that first auspicious meeting under the lilacs, the famous champion of the red and black races was no stranger in our home" (1978, p. 91). Four years later, Armstrong offered Elaine a position teaching in Hampton's nascent Indian Education department. She was 19 years old, untrained, and inexperienced with Indians, education, and most of the outside world.

By the middle of her second year teaching at Hampton, Elaine found herself "burning with an intense desire to see the much discussed and little-known 'Indian country' with [her] own eyes," and she soon after set off on a tour of Dakota Sioux Territory (Eastman & Graber, 1978, p. 2). Her memoirs detail her preparation for, and arrival at, the home territory of many of her Hampton students, whom she claimed to want to better understand via this trip. It is important to note here that Elaine compiled her memoirs herself, based on much of her published and unpublished writings over the course of several decades living among the Sioux. I note this to demonstrate that, even with decades of personal relationships with the Sioux, and marriage to a Sioux man, her characterization of the Sioux and her fight for their assimilation through education fall far short of anything one might characterize as "sisterly." Reflecting back in her old age, Eastman remarked on the surprise afforded by hindsight that someone of her age and (lack of) experience would be allowed to open and run a school in Indian Territory as "a mere girl of twenty-two who proposed to create a little center of 'sweetness and light' ... in a squalid camp of savages" at White River Camp (p. 30) where she found the Natives surprisingly humanlike, "their friendly ways and dark, smiling faces" making a "pleasant impression" (p. 25).

At the "heart of the forlorn little community" Eastman found a schoolhouse and mission residence, both unoccupied remnants of a government plan to litter "Indian Territory" with schoolhouses and teachers to help assimilate and Americanize them. Without any curiosity as to why the structures remained unoccupied, nor a mention of what made the community "forlorn" in the first place (did its inhabitants find it forlorn? Is this merely Eastman's assessment of a culture unlike her own sheltered upbringing? Was there, perhaps, any fault on the part of the US government and missionaries like herself that might have led to the forlorn nature of White River Camp?), Eastman knew at once that she had found her calling in life, heeding her mother's call for duty and service above self. She marked herself a hero, wondering rhetorically, "who would open the inhospitable doors of the waiting schoolhouse and ring the silent bells [if not her]?" (p. 26), echoing the nearly identical sentiment made by Lucy Thurston on her way to save the Kanaka Maoli of Hawai'i (see Chapter 3).

Adjacent to the abandoned schoolhouse "rose a stately new tent, handsomely decorated and protected by a neat fence of woven willows – the 'Ghost Lodge,'[17] sacred to the spirits of the honored idea" (p. 25). It was clear in the 1800s, as it is today, that the schoolhouse stood as a symbol of American assimilation, progress, and desire for entrance into a recognized humanity. Standing between the symbols of two "opposing and irreconcilable" cultures – one needed, sacred, and clearly in regular use, the other abandoned before completion – Eastman deduced that her duty, and the Sioux's need, was clear: she must take on the "selfless duty" of reclaiming, opening, and running the day school to save the Indian people in the manner she knew was right. "She had made up her mind to begin at the beginning, in the heart of a newly transplanted, leaderless, bewildered little community" (p. 29). Eastman was immediately and simultaneously a self-described expert on Indians (for white America) and what was best for Indians and the country at large: assimilation into white, Protestant, capitalist morality and existences.

Here and throughout Eastman's memoirs – most of which, we should recall, were published as articles and widely read during her early life among the Sioux[18] – she differentiates between Indian and white, savage versus human, referring to "wild men" and "their even more primitive allies" (Eastman & Graber, 1978, p. 27) versus those Indians who showed human potential through their participation in her assimilationist project. She argued, "mixed-bloods and men of better mental caliber or a smattering of education perceived clearly that the old life was at an end … These were the ones who should have been heard" (p. 88). While Sioux men were marked as subhuman and ignorant, Sioux women were described as "childlike," "lovable," "intensely feminine," "innocent," "devoted" (p. 34) as well as superstitious and simpleminded (p. 70). To clarify Eastman's self-appointed benevolence, she was an advocate for and "sister to the Sioux" who accepted their fate as an endangered people with no recourse but to attempt melting into whiteness. She was therefore not much of an advocate for Indians at all, but instead an advocate for whiteness, white supremacy, and a Protestant capitalist notion of proper American citizenry.

Eastman accepted the very doctrine that she attempted to distance herself from: that "a handful of primitives whose own way of life had been made impossible by our countrymen's advance could survive and prosper only through adaptation to the modern [white] world" (p. 22). She found no fault with this belief, nor with the genocidal impact her "countrymen's advance" made on the Indigenous tribes of North America. She in fact added her proud recollection of realizing "education was the master-key and that education must be universal" in assimilating the Indians to a white Protestant way of life. At times in her memoirs, Eastman hinted at a slight sense of sorrow or perhaps pity toward the displaced tribes she had come to "know and love," but nothing outweighed her firm belief in the superiority of the "white race" and the unavoidable doom awaiting those tribes who refused to relocate and assimilate to make way for her nation's geographic and economic progress (Eastman & Graber, 1978). Despite the generally understood 19th-century ideal of women being disempowered and required to stay in the home at the command of patriarchy, at no point in her memoirs does Eastman indicate awareness of such a standard. Rather, she retells the story of her youth and her subsequent decades among the Sioux with unwavering confidence in her early knowledge of her destiny to be out among the Indian tribes, speaking for them, and teaching them the proper ways of white womanhood and humanity in general (ironic, since the "proper womanhood" taught to Indigenous women was nothing like the womanhood Eastman embodied).

Despite her self-assigned role as expert and savior to Indians, Eastman's publications and memoirs demonstrate her commitment to aligning with the racist white supremacist ideologies of her day. Although it is true that she spent much of her adult life working on behalf of the Sioux and Indian education in general, Eastman spent little to no time letting the Sioux speak for themselves, and her advocacy was firmly rooted in a maternalistic belief in assimilating a lesser population of beings into a more enlightened/whitened identity and way of being.

She wrote about the state of Indian/white relations just before the massacre at Wounded Knee:

> We who really knew and loved the Sioux were convinced that, with patience and redress of their grievances, the sane and loyal majority might safely be counted upon to bring a fanatical few to their senses. It cannot be too clearly understood that the clash was between two cultures – not two races. The cause of the pretend Messiah was already lost and time was on our side.
>
> (Eastman & Graber, 1978, p. 155)

Regardless of her own devout belief in a Christian religion dependent upon the idea of a messianic savior returning to the Earth, Eastman repeatedly mocked Sioux beliefs in the Ghost Dance, the coming of a Native messiah, and the return of the buffalo that would signal a return of the land to North American tribes. Whereas many white men in the United States military and Indian Department were greatly concerned about a coming Indian uprising, Eastman recollected the time with the same youthful confidence that saturates all of her writing that only "a handful of hopeless and desperate men" would even consider rising up against the state, noting further that "we who loved[19] them moved among them as freely and with as much confidence as ever" (Eastman & Graber, 1978, pp. 145–146). Here again, Eastman refers to those whom she's decided had not yet reached their potential for humanity by assimilating into a white Protestant capitalist ideal. Those Indians whom Eastman granted human status were those who were, in her eyes, civilized. On a tour of reservation schools, Eastman was surprised to come across civilized people, defined as those who had adopted white Protestant ethics and lifestyles, living in homes "quite equal to those of the average [white] settler." Women who were "good house-keepers and neatly dressed" had children who were "clean and attractive," all of whom spoke English and supported Eastman's desires to open additional day schools on their land.

Supporting Eastman's identity as part of the Sioux family, she filled her contemporary publications and memoir with evidence of her selfless sacrifice and heroism, along with the common colonialist refrain of maternalistic all-knowing expertise on an otherwise un-evolved people. Not satisfied to teach Indigenous children only, Eastman insisted on teaching the adults in White River Camp as well, furthering the 19th-century belief that white women knew better than other women how to be proper women, and that they certainly knew better than nonwhite men and women when it came to parenting and properly raising decent children. Indigenous ways were discursively reduced to silly superstition and ignorance, while Eastman set about teaching men how to parent or, more often, intervening in parent–child relationships to parent by proxy the children who she deemed uncared for.

Retelling the story of a child named Scarlett Ball ("our own Florence"), Eastman decided the girl's father simply did not know any better because he refused to send his daughter to the government day school. Rather than respecting a father's wishes (which would have required her to view him as a real parent in the first place), Eastman lured Scarlett Ball to school with "baskets of inviting food" and then enrolled her on her own (Eastman & Graber, 1978, p. 42). Within two years of schooling, Scarlett was appropriately assimilated by Eastman's standards – in this case because she began pushing her father toward Christianity. Despite his refusal to convert, and based on no more than a lukewarm sentiment that his "seed had grown" from schooling, Eastman joyously announced that the "one time skeptic father is ever-grateful" for her intervention into his family, though she had bypassed his parental authority and converted a child she only lured away through trickery.

Eastman's memoirs are riddled with misunderstood retellings of Indigenous parents refusing assimilation through their children's forced education, translated as eager parents handing off their children to someone who clearly knew better. In response to Chief Medicine Bull's statement that he has sent a son and daughter to Hampton "so that they may someday come back and be my eyes," Eastman misreads his intention to use the master's tools to dismantle the master's house, using white schooling as a weapon against itself in the war for ideological colonization. Instead, she heard his words as not only an unwavering acceptance of her assimilationist methods, but also as a calling/sign from above, writing, "here was a clear call to the heart of the ardent young girl – a call which she then and there silently promised herself to answer" (Eastman & Graber, 1978, p. 26).

During a great blizzard of 1888, Eastman revealed herself and the few other white women as the sole saviors of a tribe otherwise incapable of surviving winter during which 200 Dakotans – mostly children – died. "Heroic teachers held their flock all night," she wrote, "perhaps burning desks and benches to keep from freezing ... until toward nightfall the parents appeared, amused and grateful" (Eastman & Graber, 1978, p. 47). Here and throughout her memoirs, Eastman recalls with paternalistic amusement how the very lives and existences of Dakota Sioux depended on the heroics of white womanhood while child-like and incompetent Indigenous elders sat by without acting and/or expressed immeasurable gratitude for the white women's good (better) sense.

After her brief time teaching at White River Camp, Eastman became a paid speaker and expert on Indian education, often appearing in front of US congressional committees where she found herself to be not only an expert but a hero to the Indians, positioning herself against congressmen whom, she noted, had the most "self-congratulatory ignorance" on the "Indian question" (Eastman & Graber, 1978, p. 21). One of her many examples of advocating on behalf of her beloved Native "family" and for the further financial and political support of reservation day schools included the following memory:

I retorted with a story of heavily marked features that "lighten and quicken from day to day," of "rows of dusky faces fairly alive with every variety of expression," of "odd, bright questions and answers that make knowledge which before seemed hackneyed, even to one's self, a fresh mental acquisition".

(Eastman & Graber, 1978, p. 20)

In language akin to one who had surprised herself by teaching a trained animal a new trick, Eastman propped herself up as the sole voice for Indian education and rights, all the while doubly silencing Indigenous voices during her youth and again while re-crafting her memoirs in her old age. All the while, Eastman admitted throughout her writings that she was functioning on pure instinct, pluck, and pioneering spirit in lieu of any formal training or much experience.

Yet despite her lack of qualifications, not once in her memoirs did Eastman consider that she might not know best, nor that she might in fact have been further damaging the Sioux through her insistence on erasing the very culture that she claimed to love and adopt as her own. She recalled her short journey toward obtaining an official government post overseeing Indian Education:

"When I went east again the autumn of 1889 [with less than three years' experience teaching in Dakota Sioux Territory], I had no money and no job, but I had ideas to spare and plenty of self-confidence. Believing that I knew the Sioux and their needs, I had made definite plans for my next campaign".

(Eastman & Graber, 1978, p. 114)

Those plans included working for the US government's Indian Office as a public speaker on Indian education, for which she was (and is still) widely recognized as an expert only because no one (white) knew nor attempted to know Indian life on the reservations (or anywhere else, outside of stereotypical characterizations).

At this time, General Morgan, the not-yet-confirmed appointee to the Indian Commission, publicly named Eastman as supervisor of the entire system of day schools in the Dakotas. This role was quickly expanded to "Supervisor of Education in the two Dakotas," a position created specifically for Eastman, putting her in charge of all day schools and "several large boarding schools" and catapulting her into a position of power previously unheard of for a woman (p. 116). In her new position as supervisor, Eastman was a vocal proponent of day schools over boarding schools, but not for the reasons for which she is often lauded (in short, keeping families together); rather, Eastman saw day schools for their powerful potential as tools for white supremacy and assimilation. She argued that day schools could assimilate Indian tribes more efficiently and effectively because they were more cost effective (less than half the cost of boarding schools), there would be less parental opposition to enrolling children, and most importantly, the day schools would have a greater assimilationist impact on adults and families than boarding schools that kept students away from home, often for life. Eastman's tenure as supervisor for the Dakotas required her to travel among the five Dakota reservations to supervise and evaluate more than 60 government and missionary schools, allowing her a degree of freedom and adventure that few women enjoyed in the 19th century.

Conclusion

Following her mentor and "strongest influence in [her] life" Samuel Chapman Armstrong's beliefs in Indian education and assimilation (Indians are "grown up children" and "we are a thousand years ahead of them"), Eastman became one of the most valued and powerful voices influencing Indian education and federal policy in the 19th century (Talbot, 1904, p. 277) and perhaps beyond. Her memoirs, based on her collection of letters and articles published during her earlier life, paint the picture of a benevolent hero and surrogate mother and sister to the Indigenous peoples of the Dakotas. For contemporary readers and for her contemporaries, Eastman's voice served as one of few authorities on the birth and gestation of government and missionary Indian schools. Her racist distrust toward "uncivilized" Natives is lovingly couched in language of maternalistic best practices, not unlike much of the rhetoric used in educational reform discourse of the present day; through this rhetorical turn, Eastman is lauded as a hero to Indigenous peoples as well as for a nascent white feminism.

Although she was well published and often sought out as the singular expert on Indian education, Eastman expressed deep regret that her literary career never took off as she had hoped it would. Aside from her childhood books of poetry, her most well-known writings were her husband's books on growing up as an Indian – for which Elaine Eastman has been posthumously given primary credit by those who re-inscribe her as heroic, benevolent, and superior to the Indigenous peoples she selflessly served. This discursive reiteration of near sainthood is especially common in works written by contemporary women (Alexander, 1988, 1992; Eick, 2008; Ellinghaus, 1999) as well as by her most recent biographer (Sargent, 2005). To a much broader audience, the national Public Broadcasting Station (pbs.org) includes Eastman in its online history of unquestionably heroic teachers,[20] a site which opens with the Spalding Gray quote: "Good teachers to me are like poets and saints."

While I cannot argue that countless (dare I say, even most?) teachers, past and present, have entered the profession with honorable intentions, perhaps even landing somewhere on a spectrum between poetic in skills and saintly in patience, the reiterative discursive construction of women who teach as infallibly maternal and wholly benevolent is as dangerous as it is false. The trope of teacher as savior by definition puts white women teachers in a position of binary opposition with the violent military (masculine) power that has always marched alongside the feminine missionary colonial schoolteacher, when in reality, each role operated as two arms of the same beast. To forgo a more nuanced, complex understanding of the power and violence tied to maternalistic colonialism and benevolent whiteness is to perpetuate a misunderstanding of the history of schools and schooling and teachers' roles therein. In addition, such binary positioning reinforces contemporary historical amnesia and undermines our ability to understand our roles as teachers in oppressed communities as one that has always been fraught with violence, cultural and literal genocide, the furthering of white supremacy, and a narrow definition of a precise and perfect student-subject modeled after arcane Protestant ideals. Until we are willing to engage in a thorough genealogical understanding of the power and purpose of teaching, we will remain unable to reimagine schools and teaching in a manner that is decolonial and emancipatory for those we have claimed to serve for the past two centuries.

Toward that end, throughout this book and in the following concluding chapter, I consider the questions raised throughout this historical look at benevolent whiteness and its role in furthering the power of the white nation state by way of a feminized educational system, including the following:

> What does white women's confessional literature of the 19th century demonstrate about, and what can we learn from, the ways in which white women's benevolence served them in their unorthodox performance of womanhood, their power over oppressed and colonized peoples, and their agency and influence within institutions during an era when women had little power or voice outside of the heteronormative Protestant home? What are the benefits white women get from their "good deeds" and "selfless service" while working for a violently patriarchal system that simultaneously works against them?

By weaving these connections, I ask readers to complicate their understandings of "good intentions" and to consider that their desires to serve and "save" historically oppressed students reinforce and reproduce violent white supremacy. For parents and teachers of color, again, the chapter closes with a reminder that our resistance to and refusal of settler colonial violence can be found in the ruptures in history (Foucault) as well as in our stories, genealogies, and oral histories, all of which are as valid as the traditional archives. Thus, this chapter reminds us and others that we as Black, Indigenous, and people of color are legitimate holders of knowledge and ways of learning, and as such it is our right and responsibility to determine what are "good intentions" – "culturally sustaining practices" (Paris & Alim, 2017) and politics when it comes to our own children.

Notes

1 The "Second Great Awakening" was a swell of Protestant evangelical revivalism flooding the United States in the first quarter of the 19th century. This new religious revival brought thousands of converts into the church, all fuelled with the belief that their main duties to God and man included the eradication of sin, and a dedication to Biblical perfectionism for themselves and anyone they might convert. Conversion and specifically spreading the light among dark nations was a core tenet of 19th-century evangelical Protestantism, with one's sole purpose in life being the forced conversion and salvation of all the world's peoples. In the 19th century, conversions were largely contained within New England via regional traveling preachers and large religious gatherings or "camps" during which the devout could affirm their fervor while also bringing in potential converts. Of the thousands of new converts, far more were women than men. This led to a "feminization of religion" (Zwiep, 1991, pp. 10–11) previously unseen, which occurred coincidentally alongside the feminization of the teaching profession. See Chapter 2 for a more detailed discussion.

2 I use the terms "Indian," "Native American," and "American Indian" here, and whenever I am directly quoting or referring to a 19th-century term, such as Native American boarding schools. "Indigenous Peoples" will be used when I am speaking in my own voice, especially when referring to Indigenous Peoples collectively/globally. When tribal affiliation is known, I use self-identified tribal names unless directly quoting an author or archival source.

3 The "Indian problem" refers to Indigenous tribes "owning" land desired by white settlers; the problem or question was, in short, whether nor not this problem would be rectified by Indigenous genocide or assimilation.

4 The "common school movement" was a reform movement led by Horace Mann, then-secretary of education in Massachusetts. The movement quickly spread throughout the United States with the goal of providing a basic taxpayer-funded education for all (white) students. See Chapter 1 for fuller treatment of the common school movement in relation to the feminization of teaching.

5 U.S. Statutes at Large, 3:516–517.

6 It is also important to point out that most tribes had well-established agricultural traditions that were not acknowledged by reformers, likely because (1) agricultural work was largely women's work, and (2) Indigenous agricultural methods did not depend on European tools and strategies.

7 Sometimes referred to as the Office of Indian Affairs, a term preferred by department head Thomas McKenney.

8 For a thorough explanation of Calhoun's involvement in unilaterally creating the Bureau of Indian Affairs, see Belko, W. (2004). "John C. Calhoun and the Creation of the Bureau of Indian Affairs: An essay on political rivalry, ideology, and policymaking in the early republic." *The South Carolina Historical Magazine, 105*(3), 170–197.

9 U.S. Statutes at Large, 3:516–17.

10 Subgroups included the Women's National Indian Association, the Indian Rights Association, and the National Indian Defence Association (Bannan, 1978, p. 788).

11 Some girls were allowed to attend schools, but their education differed and focused primarily on home economics and raising "good boys" who would grow up to be good republican citizens.

12 In some places, Baltimore for example, educated slaves were a boon to their white owners, whereas in New England educated free Blacks were seen as direct economic competition to white men. For an excellent exploration of the complexity of Black education in the prewar United States, see Moss, *Schooling citizens: The struggle for African American education in antebellum America*, and Jones, *Soldiers of light and love: Northern teachers and Georgia Blacks, 1865–1873*.

13 Washington was more concerned with economic development; Du Bois was concerned with education of all, especially the "talented 10th" who might uplift the race. Washington's schools focused on self-sufficiency: students built their own schools, focused on growing food, and so on. Du Bois wanted Black students held to the same academic standards as whites; taking classical courses such as Latin and Greek.

14 This is not meant to further the factually reductive dichotomy of Du Bois versus Washington in the struggle for Black resistance against white supremacy during this era; however, for the purposes of this project there is not sufficient space to address this topic to the degree necessary to do it justice. For an excellent analysis of the complexity of Black resistance at the turn of the 20th century, see Glenda Elizabeth Gilmore's 1996 book *Gender and Jim Crow: Women and the politics of white supremacy in North Carolina, 1896–1920*. Chapel Hill: University of North Carolina Press.

15 S.C. Armstrong to Richard Baxter Armstrong, dated 12 December 1862.

16 Pratt's now-famous quote was first spoken while reading a paper at an 1892 convention. Source: Official Report of the Nineteenth Annual Conference of Charities and Correction (1892), 46–59. Reprinted in Pratt, R.H. (1873). "The Advantages of Mingling Indians with Whites," *Americanizing the American Indians: Writings by the "Friends of the Indian" 1880–1900*. Cambridge, MA: Harvard University Press, 260–271.

17 The "ghost lodge" was an English misnomer for the ceremonial Sioux sweat lodge.

18 She writes during her first visit to Indian Country, "my letters from the field, hurriedly written in longhand with no opportunity to polish, were already appearing in New York and Boston papers … they described in detail the semi barbaric spectacle of Indian camp and council, new to most readers, not forgetting to stress the effects of mission training with its promise for the future" (Eastman & Graber, 1978, p. 28).

19 See Chapter 1 for an in-depth exploration of the use of love language as a feminized form of colonial violence.

20 http://www.pbs.org/onlyateacher/about.html.

References

Alexander, R. A. (1988). Elaine Goodale Eastman and the failure of the feminist Protestant ethic. *Great Plains Quarterly*, 8(2), 89–101.

Alexander, R. A. (1992). Finding oneself through a cause: Elaine Goodale Eastman and Indian reform in the 1880s. *South Dakota History*, 22, 1–37.

Anderson, J. D. (1988). *The education of Blacks in the South, 1860–1935*. Chapel Hill: University of North Carolina Press.

Bannan, H. M. (1978). The idea of civilization and American Indian policy reformers in the 1880s. *Journal of American Culture*, 1, 787–799.

Belko, W. (2004). John C. Calhoun and the creation of the Bureau of Indian Affairs: An essay on political rivalry, ideology, and policymaking in the early republic. *The South Carolina Historical Magazine*, 105(3), 170–197.

Butchart, R. E. (1980). *Northern schools, southern Blacks, and Reconstruction: Freedmen's education, 1862–1875*. Westport: Greenwood Press.

Eastman, E. G., & Graber, K. (1978). *Sister to the Sioux: The memoirs of Elaine Goodale Eastman, 1885–91*. Lincoln: University of Nebraska Press.

Eick, G. C. (2008). U.S. Indian policy, 1865–1890 as illuminated through the lives of Charles A Eastman and Elaine Goodale Eastman. *Great Plains Quarterly*, 28(1), 27–47.

Ellinghaus, K. (1999). Reading the personal as political: the assimilationist views of a white woman married to a Native American man, 1880s–1940s. *Australasian Journal of American Studies*, 18(2), 23–42.

Gilmore, G. E. (1996). *Gender and Jim Crow: Women and the politics of white supremacy in North Carolina, 1896–1920.* Chapel Hill: University of North Carolina Press.

Hampton Institute. (1893). *Twenty-two years' work of the Hampton Normal and Agricultural Institute at Hampton, Virginia: Records of Negro and Indian graduates and ex-students, with historical and personal sketches and testimony on important race questions from within and without; to which are added … some of the songs of the races gathered in the school.* Hampton: Normal School Press.

Katznelson, I., & Weir, M. (1988). *Schooling for all: Class, race, and the decline of the democratic ideal.* Berkeley: University of California Press.

Keller, C. (2000). Philanthropy betrayed: Thomas Jefferson, the Louisiana Purchase, and the origins of federal Indian removal policy. *Proceedings of the American Philosophical Society, 144*(1), 39–66. Retrieved from http://www.jstor.org/stable/1515604

King, D. (2000). *Making Americans: Immigration, race, and the origins of the diverse democracy.* Cambridge, MA: Harvard.

Mann, H. (1848). Report no. 12 of the Massachusetts school board. *The Republic and the School: Horace Mann on the education of free men,* 415–449.

Pratt, R. H. (1873). The Advantages of Mingling Indians with Whites. In Francis Paul Prucha (ed.), *Americanizing the American Indians: Writings by the "Friends of the Indian" 1880–1900* (pp. 260–271). Cambridge, MA: Harvard University Press.

Richardson, J. M. (2009). *Christian reconstruction: The American Missionary Association and southern Blacks, 1861–1890.* Athens: University of Alabama Press.

Sargent, T. D. (2005). *The life of Elaine Goodale Eastman.* Lincoln: University of Nebraska Press. Retrieved September 16, 2016, from Project MUSE database. http://muse.jhu.edu/book/11744

Spring, J. (2016). *Deculturalization and the struggle for equality: A brief history of the education of dominated cultures in the United States.* Abingdon: Routledge.

Talbot, E. A. (1904). *Samuel Chapman Armstrong: A biographical study.* New York, NY: Doubleday, Page & Company.

Tyack, D. B. (2003). *Seeking common ground: Public schools in a diverse society.* Cambridge, MA: Harvard University Press.

Worcester v. Georgia, 31 U.S. 515 (1832). Justia Law. Retrieved March 27, 2022, from https://supreme.justia.com/cases/federal/us/31/515/

Wu, J. (2009). Kill the Indian, Save the Man. In *The Pennsylvania Center for the Book.* Retrieved December 3, 2016, from http://pabook2.libraries.psu.edu/palitmap/CarlisleIndianSchool.html

Zwiep, M. (1991). *Pilgrim path: The first company of women missionaries to Hawai'i.* Madison: University of Wisconsin Press.

5

A WOMAN'S WORK IS NEVER DONE

Benevolent Whiteness in "Post-Racial" America

> Our mission is to enlist, develop, and mobilize as many as possible of our nation's most promising future leaders to grow and strengthen the movement for educational equity and excellence.[1]

This 2017 Teach For America (TFA) mission statement echoes 19th-century missionary ambitions with haunting similarity. Not unlike the American Board of Commissioners for Foreign Missions (ABCFM) and later the American Missionary Association (AMA), contemporary "alternative preparation" programs such as TFA aim to send their recruits to spread light to dark places across North America and the Pacific. Steeped in the language of love, selfless service, and heroics ("You have bold ambitions to make a difference. You are ready to be part of something big. Greatness is waiting on you."),[2] modern missionaries commit to teaching in areas the organization has designated as "high priority," generally low-income urban centers and rural outposts populated with children of color. The rhetoric of expert benevolent whiteness is alive and well in TFA recruitment materials, as well as in the countless blogs and memoirs written by its founder and alumni.[3] Counternarratives written by alumni of color are slowly becoming more plentiful and readily available to a wider audience of their peers, unlike the one-sided amplification of benevolent whiteness published in the 19th century. Yet in this era once proclaimed as "post-racial America"[4] the basic tenets of benevolent whiteness persist in common discourse on what it means to be an all-knowing, purely benevolent, outsider teacher in communities that are deemed "in need" of enlightenment. The dominant narrative of benevolence drowns out the voices of TFA critics; in fact, an entire public relations department at TFA is dedicated to spinning counternarratives as the voices of a few lone, maligned defectors representing a minuscule percentage of TFA alumni, or

DOI: 10.4324/9781003201809-6

as defenders of the old guard who are resisting the "relentless pursuit" of positive change that TFA represents.

As was the case with the 19th-century AMA and other "benevolent societies," government funding and public and private donors pour money into the TFA coffers during a time in which the nation's most struggling public schools (predominantly those of color) are being financially drained through the loss of state and federal funding, fines related to "failing" at high-stakes assessments, charter schools and "school choice" vouchers, and a general societal disinvestment in public schooling. The money follows the message of benevolent, all-knowing salvation, particularly rewarding the reiteration of an unwavering belief in an American bootstrap mentality and a false nostalgia for a time when schools gave everyone a "fair shot" at the American Dream. In this regard, the 21st-century message of benevolent whiteness and the functions of federal government and private funds harkens back to the Reconstruction-era South, during which already established Black schools were left unfunded while money flooded into AMA schools. Similarly, TFA-led privatization efforts and alumni-led charter schools strategically displace Black and Indigenous teachers and already-established public schools (the most drastic example of this occurring in 2005 post–Hurricane Katrina New Orleans, which is now almost completely devoid of traditional public schools). The narrative of benevolent white middle-class salvation, led by a living replica of Columbia herself, TFA founder and CEO Wendy Kopp, seeks to fulfill its manifest destiny to "One Day" create a future in which "all children in this nation will have the opportunity to attain an excellent education," as long as "excellence" remains narrowly defined through a lens of middle-class whiteness. Despite the passing of time and the changing of social and political values and ideals, the persistence of white supremacy couched in heroism remains the same. As white supremacy is the foundation upon which stands the metaphoric US home, white womanhood is merely the paint, the stucco, the brick or wood siding; while it looks different in different eras, it remains a protective layer holding up an otherwise rotten structure.

In the previous chapters, I have detailed the ways in which benevolent whiteness remained beholden to the white racial state: schools earned funding and white women earned agency and power in exchange for their service in the "army of whiteness" (Leonardo & Boas, 2013). In this chapter, I ask the reader to consider the ways in which white womanhood continues to participate in this white racial economy, collecting the "wages of whiteness" (Du Bois, 1903/1989) that afford white women positions of power within a larger patriarchal structure. Acknowledging that we no longer operate entirely under the Victorian "Cult of True Womanhood,"[5] and thus the construction of womanhood has necessarily changed as decades have passed, a genealogical understanding of its influence in the discursive construction of benevolent whiteness allows us a lens through which to examine the role of white womanhood contemporarily.

In this concluding this book, I consider the implications for this study, particularly in relation to training a new generation of teachers that continues to be predominantly white and female. In this era that until recently was lauded as "post-racial," during which #BlackLivesMatter signs and swag are common sights in businesses, schools, and communities, and during which you can no longer attend an event without hearing a performative land acknowledgment, benevolent whiteness continues to function, although arguably in a mutated form, in contemporary women's writings as well as through "alternative" teaching programs like Teach For America (as well as in traditional teacher education programs – a topic worthy of its own entire book). White womanhood continues to operate through hidden wages of whiteness, hidden under its cloak of invisible normativity, innocence, and perpetual victimhood under patriarchy. The collective national discourse on teaching and teachers in "underserved" or "urban" schools remains focused on inherent benevolence and heroism, a chorus perpetually singing the praises of those who dare to do this "thankless" and seemingly impossible work for toward the uplift of oppressed peoples and thus the betterment of the nation. Benevolent whiteness in our schools persists, with little interrogation into the possibility that teachers might have good intentions that nevertheless result in malevolent outcomes.

This chapter concludes the book by asking us to consider how and why benevolent whiteness persists, particularly in our schools, and how each of us plays a role in either upholding or interrupting it. Regardless of whether teachers' uptake of benevolent whiteness is intentional, or if it is the residual effect of centuries of conditioning and normalization, the task ahead of those of us who strive to work toward emancipatory education is to persistently ask ourselves and our colleagues and coconspirators how benevolent whiteness can be located and dislocated in contemporary classrooms and teacher preparation programs.

Toward that end, I want to revisit the theoretical and practical questions that inspired this project over a decade ago. As a classroom teacher and instructional coach in a variety of "progressive" private, charter, and public schools in the Bay Area, I sat through meeting after meeting about our schools' "discipline gap": the disproportionally high numbers of Black kids we suspended despite Black students representing a small fraction of our overall student population. In these meetings, regardless of what collection of progressive (predominantly white) educators filled the room, the focus always centered the children, their families, their deficiencies or "unique conditions" that caused them to get suspended – as if it were entirely by the students' choice! We collectively nodded in agreement that this was a problem in need of immediate solutions. We were anti-racist progressive educators, after all! We needed to figure out how to get students of color to change to fit into whiteness, and for their own good in the short- and long-term futures. However, the conversation never centered on teachers' roles in exclusionary punishment for transgressions that were categorized more than half the time as "willful defiance." For example, many such transgressions included coming to class without materials, not dressing in the proper uniform for PE, refusing to follow an order, and other such behaviors that are certainly frustrating, especially the more they are repeated by the same child. And yet they are just that: minor annoyances. They are things that pushed our buttons, that called into question our absolute power as teachers, that refused our attempts at controlling and disciplining individual student subjects in the manner that we deemed best, and they were punished by excluding from the classroom the very students we aimed to "save."

This book is the result of the decades I spent working in public schools in many capacities, and my frustration with the perpetual focus on eternally unsavable Black and Brown students by predominantly white teachers. This frustration and a desire to change the lens through which we view things like racist student discipline trends enforced by teachers who "love their students" landed me in a doctoral program where I began to ask the following questions, work that grew over a decade into this book: What does it mean, and how is it useful to conceptualize white women as agents and schools as sites of white supremacy? How does genealogical understanding of gendered whiteness (in relation to gendered settler colonialism) allow for a more nuanced understanding of contemporary teacher identities and raced and gendered relationships in schools? How viable is a theory of gendered benevolent whiteness given the fluidity and performative nature of both whiteness and gender? How might we understand the contemporary (over)disciplining of Black and Brown youth as a consequence of what have been historically framed as benevolent intentions enacted through what is essentially feminized white supremacy? These questions, as my research reveals, can indeed help us to construct a genealogy of benevolent whiteness: a backward mapping of the settler colonial origins behind the contemporary trope of the heroic white woman who will save our schools. From such a standpoint, teachers and teacher educators can begin to (re)construct both our complicity and emancipatory potential within schools and the larger US settler colonial project. I address the questions directly and briefly here:

What Does It Mean, and How Is It Useful to Conceptualize White Women as Agents and Schools as Sites of White Supremacy? How Does a Genealogical Understanding of Gendered Whiteness Allow for a More Nuanced Understanding of Contemporary Teacher Identities and Raced/Gendered Relationships in Schools?

Zeus Leonardo (2013) reminds us that under the tenets of Critical Whiteness Studies (CWS) it is whiteness, and not people of color, that needs changing, and therefore there will always be a limit to the possibilities of educational research and policy that insist we focus on "fixing" pathologized communities of color. Nevertheless, that is where far too much educational research focuses its efforts: toward understanding what makes Black and Brown youth prone to behaviors that result in their failure in and necessary removal from schools. Instead of wondering "what is the problem with whiteness?" (or proposing that it is itself the problem), we ask what it is about Blackness that resists the mold of proper student subjectivity and how can we better help nonwhite students to "fit in" to a mold constructed on a model of 19th-century whiteness. A gendered interrogation into whiteness in schools is lacking: the literature on white womanhood lacks a focus on schooling, particularly a focus on the relationship between schooling and "disciplining," in both the traditional and the Foucauldian senses of the word, and the ever-expanding work on whiteness in education remains suspiciously gender-neutral. As such, CWS alone does not get us as far as we need to go in understanding the ways in which an explicitly feminized whiteness has been employed within sites understood as women's "places" (schools and home, specifically). An Indigenous feminist genealogical method as outlined in Chapter 1 provides an understanding of benevolent whiteness, which in turn offers a more precise lens through which to understand the nuances of gendered white supremacy within a patriarchal culture at large and within schooling in specific.

Understanding the role of benevolent whiteness in furthering white supremacy and the settler colonial state requires an acceptance of whiteness as something other than normative and invisible to begin with, which this book proposes can begin via a genealogical understanding of its obstruction and persistence. Toward this end, it is first necessary to acknowledge the United States as a settler colonial state, and the history of schools as intentional sites of settler colonial white supremacy working in service of the state. Additionally, we must make visible and interrogate the roles white women have played in the perpetuation of settler colonialism, particularly during the founding decades of systematized schooling. As I have demonstrated, the conflation of 19th-century white middle-class mothering with the feminization of teaching has resulted in the discursive construction of teaching as inherently benevolent, and by that rationale as exempt from critique within the larger settler colonial project. It is thus necessary that contemporary educators and researchers locate teachers, the majority of whom are white women, as always already imbued with extraordinary power and agency within (and thus culpability for the ramifications of) US white supremacy and its settler colonial schools, past and present. Further, this more nuanced conceptualization of white womanhood allows for – in fact requires – contemporary teachers to locate themselves within a larger project, as deeply entangled in the erratic web of white supremacy, and thus to consider ongoing educational problems such as the "discipline gap" through this lens, rather than allowing them a "pass" for being well intentioned and "not racist."

How Viable Is a Theory of Gendered Benevolent Whiteness Given the Fluidity and Performative Nature of Both Whiteness and Gender?

It is now well established that gender is as fluid as it is performative (Butler, 1988), despite the "colonial imposition of gender binaries" (Lugones, 2010) on colonized peoples. Because this book understands whiteness as ideological, I propose that whiteness, to a certain degree, can be as fluid and performative as gender. Through this claim, I am signaling the ways in which whiteness is used and reinforced by people of color, particularly within a school system that is rooted in inescapable and compulsory whiteness. Therefore, to define benevolent whiteness as gendered female does not imply that its invocation is restricted to cis-gendered women who are genotypically or phenotypically marked as "white people." The theorization of benevolent whiteness allows teachers and scholars a lens through which to view educational inequities and institutional racism as the result of an unstable foundation upon which we have all agreed (to varying degrees) to build our schools.

How Can We Understand the Contemporary Over-Disciplining of Black and Brown Youth as a Consequence of Benevolent Whiteness (Gendered Settler Colonialism and White Supremacy)?

Widely cited, Patrick Wolfe (2006) posits that settler colonialism requires a "logic of elimination" – the elimination of Indigenous peoples – to provide white settlers with access to valuable land. Relatedly, genocidal settler colonialism employs an "organizing grammar of race" that racializes Indigenous peoples and Black people in opposing, but related, ways, carefully controlling who is brought into or perpetually distanced from whiteness.[6] To achieve these ends, the United States legally codified Indigenous erasure and Black perpetuity and fungibility both in the "one-drop rule" (also known as the "rule of hypodescent") and in blood quantum regulations that limit Indigenous identity and access to land, both of which result in the creation of more "property" (humans and land) for white settlers. Through the theorization of settler colonialism, we see that anti-Blackness and Indigenous genocide are always already interrelated.

Benevolent whiteness, as the feminized arm of settler colonialism and white supremacy, commits the maternalistic and "loving" violence that complements the more overt, masculinized violence of military occupation and war. In educational settings, this is largely carried out through the disciplining – literally and in the Foucauldian sense – of inherently delinquent (Foucault, 1977) student subjects. As demonstrated in previous chapters, 19th-century white women were charged with disciplining nonwhite students (and parents) through middle-class Victorian codes of morality and propriety, a task carried out through informal and formalized schooling. Much of what is understood contemporarily as "proper" student behavior and the role of white teachers in educating students of color remains influenced by this historical construction. Through this logic, I argue that the current "over-disciplining" of students of color is in fact a continuation of "just disciplining" students of color – that is, there is no "over" in terms of what is intended by and necessary for white supremacy, although statistically speaking there is a dangerous over-representation of students of color punished by exclusionary discipline.

Implications: What Comes Next?

The goal of this book and its implications for the field of educational research and teacher preparation are to construct a genealogical understanding of the contemporary discourse and collective cultural understanding of white women teaching students of color as inherently heroic. The aim, thus, is to locate the historical roots of this trope to dispel the possibility of it ever having been, or ever having the potential to be, a realistic possibility for white teachers in settler colonial schools. In no uncertain terms, this book implicates white teachers in the perpetuation of white supremacy. Specifically, it locates an extraordinary amount of power and complicity in benevolent whiteness, defined in prior chapters as a gendered female (feminine) enactment of white supremacy carried out through the seemingly benevolent work of loving, mothering teacher-saviors. I would be remiss to make such a claim without also acknowledging that white teachers can be extraordinary teachers in communities of color, as there are far too many who fit that bill within my social and professional circles alone. However, as the scholarship and lived experience of people of color remind us, whiteness remains marked as normative within educational settings just as it does in the larger US social and cultural context. Therefore, even the purest intentions when based upon white middle-class lived or imagined experience and knowledge tend to have reverberating harmful effects on students of color. Given that the teaching force in the United States has been predominantly white and female for the past 150 years, the primary goal in improving educational outcomes for students of color should be to recruit and retain teachers of color in equal proportion to student populations. At the same time, and because current numbers demonstrate an increase in white women enrolled in teacher preparation programs, our secondary goal must be a collective working away from whiteness, rooted in the theoretical understanding of whiteness as "*nothing but* oppressive and false" (Roediger, 1994), along with a re-education on the history of teachers and schooling in the settler colonial United States. This requires an entirely new practice in teacher education, and in teaching, diverging and divesting from the decades-old trends toward "multiculturalism," or even the hot topic of 2021 "anti-racism."

Sleeter's (2004) study of multicultural education and white teachers' construction of race argued that attempting to "solve racism by educating whites" doesn't result in anti-racist education or in a change in teachers' understandings of race and racism. This claim is based on a series of studies ranging from the late 1970s to the early 1990s, including a two-year study by Haberman and Post (1992) in which it was found that "teacher education reinforced, rather than reconstructed, how the white students viewed children of color" (Sleeter, 2004, p. 158). Neither behavioral patterns nor self-reported perspectives on race, racism, and people of color were found to change in response to "multicultural" education. Nevertheless, I would argue that (1) the goal of teacher education is not necessarily to "solve racism" and (2) perhaps the ways in which the researchers went about "educating whites" might be a causal factor in the studies' failures. That is, the studies in question, and multiculturalism in general, aim to effect change within a predominantly white profession through educating white people about *other* peoples, cultures, and histories. Problematically, this still locates the basis of structural and reproductive racism in schools as somehow related to white people not knowing enough about "others," rather than, as I am advocating, white people not knowing enough about whiteness. As such, multicultural education remains ineffective, lacking the necessary complexity and nuance as well as the historical grounding that might otherwise provide white teachers with an understanding of themselves. This is particularly relevant as Sleeter (2004) along with Haberman and Post (1992) have demonstrated that white teachers' perceptions about people of color are based on understandings reinforced over multiple generations; white teachers' beliefs about people of color are part of the fabric of their culture, inherited unnoticed, and thus resistant to change.

Sleeter's extensive work on whiteness in education provides a necessary starting point for white teachers, written by a white teacher in a demonstration of solidarity lacking in educational literature. Meanwhile, this book is intended to push the discussion among white teachers and teacher educators both deeper and inward. The work to be done is not about white teachers knowing more about communities of color, our cultures, our ways of being and producing knowledge, and so on. Quite contrary, the work ahead of us requires white teachers paying more attention to whiteness, its history, its malignancy, its permanence within the ways in which we understand teachers, students, and the purposes of schooling. At the risk of alienating much of the teaching profession, I believe it may also require that the most "abolitionist" and "anti-racist" of white teachers commit to teaching white students the remainder of their careers.

Moving Forward: Reimagining White Teachers in Communities of Color

This book has put forth a genealogy of benevolent whiteness that has long depended upon white women as active agents in settler colonialism and as the storytellers behind the discursive construction of a persistent and dangerous trope of their own selfless heroism. One of the many malevolent effects resulting from this self-defined benevolence has been the well-documented racialized discipline gap and the pathologizing of students and communities of color. Given that the teaching force remains predominantly white and female, and remembering that teachers of color, too, are usually raised in a K–16 school system that is steeped in ideological whiteness, the task of reimagining schools and teaching can feel impossible.

It should go without saying that diversifying the teaching force is imperative, though that is a long-term and complex project. In the short term, however, it is within our immediate power to acknowledge the homogeneity of the teaching profession, particularly in relation to the rapid diversification of the US student body. We can and should expect US teacher credential programs to insist that their candidates understand the problematic history of the profession they seek to enter and the ways in which structures put in place nearly 200 years ago persist into the present day. Toward that end, we should demand that credential programs claiming to focus on preparing teachers for "urban schools" reimagine their curriculum through a lens of problematizing the normative nature of whiteness rather than problematizing the communities they seek to serve. That is to say, we should turn on its head the programmatic emphasis on understanding students of color as the primary imperative, focusing instead on understanding the teacher as self via understanding whiteness as ideology, white womanhood as identity, and settler colonialism as the structure that upholds and is upheld by both.

Likewise, we can reimagine the site-based professional development of current and veteran teachers to reflect the same focus. As a former classroom teacher of nearly a decade, I cannot count the number of faculty meetings I attended during which we analyzed our suspension data disaggregated by race and gender. Yet each time – in the most progressive cities of the most progressive state – we never got past an understanding of data that analyzed only half of the people involved: the students of color. School leaders must be responsible for guiding their teachers toward making sense of punishment data by understanding not only the child's behavior but also the teacher's identity, their understanding of what makes a "proper" student, the types of behaviors that consistently push a teacher's buttons, and whether or not "offenses" are really punishable ones, and how all of this is tied up in racism, classism, and patriarchy.

On a policy level, districts and states can follow California's example[7] and remove catchall infractions like "willful defiance" from their list of punishable offenses while also supporting an increase in positive behavioral interventions such as restorative justice. Reducing the types of behaviors and being as concise as possible in describing the remaining behaviors that may result in exclusionary punishment will drastically reduce the statistical over-punishment of students of color. This rectifies to a degree the data that show suspensions result in a reduction in learning time for students, and an increase in likelihood of dropping out and ending up in the criminal justice system.

Likewise, a move toward restorative justice requires conflict resolution through conversation and a deeper understanding of what led to both the student and the teacher getting to a point where the student is at risk of being removed from the classroom. When done correctly, there is no student–teacher power dynamic in a restorative justice conversation, and adults as well as children are asked to take responsibility for their parts in a conflict. Such an intervention offers an opportunity for teachers to regularly interrogate their roles in student–teacher conflict, and to look at their own patterns of reactions to student behavior. With an added understanding of schools as sites of systematized white supremacy, students and teachers can be supported in a deeper and more meaningful understanding of power, race, whiteness, and most importantly each other.

Ultimately, the immediate onus is on white teachers to suspend their belief in teaching as a heroic act – a difficult task given the rhetoric and history that preaches otherwise. The long-term goal toward reimagining education and de-norming whiteness requires a dramatic reimagining of schooling, including creating the material and structural supports needed to exponentially increase the number of teachers of color. However, given the present and persistent homogeneity of the teaching profession, we must first understand benevolent whiteness as something historically created and discursively reiterated and upheld. From that vantage point, we can then productively unsettle and refocus current discussions on the over-disciplining of students of color and the related pathologizing of communities of color, toward an inward reflection of individual teachers and a structural analysis of our inherently racist systems.

> The future is a realm we have inhabited for thousands of years … Come join us.
>
> – Bryan Kamaoli Kuwada (2015)

I imagine this book speaks differently to teachers who identify as Black, Indigenous, and people of color (BIPOC). What I suggest above is nothing that has not been said by BIPOC educators, parents, students, and communities for generations. Despite centuries of violence and oppression, Black and Indigenous communities have persistently valued education for its emancipatory potential, a potential to which most of our public schools are not measuring up. We continue to work within and outside of the settler state's systems to carry ourselves and our communities toward freedom; the creativity of our communities and our educational leaders, the love and joy that grow in the places where we are given agency (or taking it by force) to cultivate our people, our lāhui, ourselves in this regard knows no bounds. But to be clear we are not resigned to settler futurities that require our relentless swimming upstream to work against our erasure from both the past and the future. Because of that, we too need a way forward – collective guidance toward futures that leave the settler state behind to collapse in on itself, as it undoubtedly will. In that spirit, I conclude this chapter and this book with an imperative that any real possibilities for anticolonial/anti-racist/emancipatory education must be envisioned through the interrelated lenses of Black and Indigenous futurity and led by our communities themselves.

Indigeneity and Blackness in the United States are predicated on erasure in order to guarantee "settler futurity" (Tuck & Gaztambide-Fernández, 2013). Black and Indigenous peoples have been erased from the past and future through settler colonial violence ranging from literal physical death, enforcement of blood quantum laws, and removal from our lands. In schools, symbolic erasure is enacted through pedagogical indoctrination and Americanization, the banning of our languages and cultural practices; corporeal erasure occurs in racist disciplinary practices that remove our children from classrooms and eventually from the school system entirely; and we have been quite literally erased from what is written about US history, from Texas textbook publishers reinventing slavery as just another type of labor, to the persistence of rhetoric that teaches students about primitive and savage Indigenous peoples who "once lived" in the distant past.

Conversely, Black and Indigenous futurity is an epistemology through which we make indelible Black and Indigenous existence now and in the future. Examples of advancing Black and Indigenous futurities can be seen in movements for Black lives, fights for rematriation of stolen land and protections of global waters, in the years-long effort to protect Mauna a Wākea, in what Noelani Goodyear-Kaʻōpua (2017) explains are ways we are "protecting the possibilities of multiple futures" inspired by our knowledge of the past. In educational spaces, futurity is enacted formally and informally through the creation of Native Hawaiian cultural schools, to elders preserving and passing on Indigenous languages that the United States sought to eradicate, to the community-based BIPOC homeschooling movements that existed before Covid and that have flourished during the ongoing pandemic (as of this writing we are completing its second year with no end in sight). Through futurity as an epistemological stance, we make visible and viable for ourselves worlds where our freedom and futures do not depend on an end to setter colonialism. Instead, we reveal a reality outside of settler colonialism where we always already not only exist but thrive, experience joy, perpetuate our cultures, protect our nonhuman relatives and our lands, and experience love and education for emancipation rather than as means to control us. Moving forward, it is this world I am focused on imagining for my children and for yours.

Notes

1 https://www.teachforamerica.org/about-us/our-mission.
2 https://www.teachforamerica.org.
3 *Cf.* Kopp, W. (2008) *One day, all children: The unlikely triumph of Teach For America and what I learned along the way*, and *A chance to make history: What works and what doesn't in providing an excellent education for all;* Sockel, H. (2015) *The kids don't stand a chance: Growing up in Teach for America;* Foote, D. (2008) Relentless Pursuit; Copperman, M. (2016) *Teacher: Two years in the Mississippi Delta;* Ness, M. (2004) *Lessons to learn: Voices from the frontlines of Teach for America.*
4 After the first election of President Barack Obama (2008), much public discourse reductively lauded the landmark occasion as an entry into a new "post-racial" era; in 2021, still reeling from four years of the neo-fascist Trump administration, we would be hard-pressed to argue that the post-racial misnomer extends to the present.
5 See Chapter 1 for an explanation of the "Cult of True Womanhood" and its role in missionary service and the feminization of teaching.
6 See Maile Arvin's (2019) *Possessing Polynesians: The Science of Settler Colonial Whiteness in Hawai`i and Oceania* for a brilliant analysis of the "near whiteness" of Polynesians.
7 California recently (2019) banned "willful defiance" as a suspendable offense up to grade 5, and for grades 6–8 it has been banned for a five-year trial period. Individual school districts within California have banned the category across all grade levels.

References

Arvin, M. R. (2019). *Possessing polynesians: The science of settler colonial whiteness in Hawai`i and Oceania.* Durham: Duke University Press.

Butler, J. (1988). Performative acts and gender constitution: An essay in phenomenology and feminist theory. *Theatre Journal, 40*(4), 519–531.

Copperman, M. (2016). *Teacher: Two years in the Mississippi Delta.* Jackson: Mississippi University Press.

Du Bois, W. E. B. (1903/1989). *The souls of black folk: Essays and sketches.* New York, NY: Penguin Books. Chicago, A. G. McClurg, 1903. New York, NY: Johnson Reprint Corp.

Foote, D. (2008). *Relentless pursuit: A year in the trenches with Teach for America.* New York, NY: Alfred A. Knopf.

Foucault, M. (1977). *Discipline and punish: The birth of the prison.* New York, NY: Vintage Books.

Goodyear-Ka`ōpua, N. (2017). Protectors of the future, not protestors of the past: Indigenous Pacific activism and Mauna a Wākea. *South Atlantic Quarterly, 116*(1), 184–194.

Haberman, M., & Post, L. (1992). Does direct experience change education students' perceptions of low-income minority children. *Mid-Western Educational Researcher, 5*(2), 29–31.

Kopp, W. (2008). *One day, all children: The unlikely triumph of Teach for America and what I learned along the way.* New York, NY: Public Affairs.

Kuwada, Bryan Kamaoli. "We live in the future. Come join us." *Ke Kaupu Hehi Ale,* July 7, 2015. Retrieved from https://hehiale.com/2015/04/03/we-live-in-the-future-come-join-us/

Leonardo, Z. (2013). *Race frameworks: A multidimensional theory of racism and education.* New York, NY: Teachers College

Leonardo, Z., & Boas, E. (2013). Other kids' teachers: What children of color learn from white women and what this says about race, whiteness, and gender. In Marvin Lynn & Adrienne D. Dixson (eds.), *Handbook of critical race theory in education* (pp. 313–324). New York: Routledge.

Lugones, M. (2010). Toward a decolonial feminism. *Hypatia, 25*(4), 742–759.

Ness, M., & Teach for America (Project). (2004). *Lessons to learn: Voices from the frontlines of Teach for America.* New York, NY: Routledge Falmer.

Roediger, D. (1994). *Toward the abolition of whiteness.* New York, NY: Verso.

Sleeter, C. E. (2004). How white teachers construct race. In David Gillborn & Gloria Ladson-Billings (eds.), *The RoutledgeFalmer reader in multicultural education* (pp. 163–178). London: RoutledgeFalmer.

Sockel, H. (2015). *The kids don't stand a chance: Growing up in Teach for America.* Seattle, WA: Amazon Digital Services LLC.

Tuck, E., & Gaztambide-Fernández, R. A. (2013). Curriculum, replacement, and settler futurity. *Journal of Curriculum Theorizing, 29*(1), 72–89.

Wolfe, P. (2006). Settler Colonialism and the Elimination of the Native. *Journal of Genocide Research, 8*(4), 387–409.

INDEX